A Brief Introduction to Hinduism

A Brief Introduction to
HINDUISM

Updated and revised by Tim Dowley

General Editor: Christopher Partridge

Fortress Press

Minneapolis

A BRIEF INTRODUCTION TO HINDUISM

The maps and images on pages 92-94 appear in *Atlas of World Religions* (Fortress Press,
forthcoming).

Cover image: Colorful patterns of the old paintings, flowers and decor on wooden
ceiling of Buddha ancient temple/iStock.com/Radiokukka; Indian Hindu God Sri
Krishna wooden carving/iStock.com/Reddees
Cover design: Laurie Ingram

Print ISBN: 978-1-5064-5034-6
eBook ISBN: 978-1-5064-5035-3

Manufactured in the USA

CONSULTING EDITORS

Contents

PART 1
UNDERSTANDING RELIGION

PART 2
HINDUISM

Contributors

Dr Fiona Bowie, Honorary Research Fellow, Department of Archaeology and Anthropology, University of Bristol, UK: *The Anthropology of Religion, Ritual and Performance*

Dr Jeremy Carrette, Professor of Religion and Culture, University of Kent, England: *Critical Theory and Religion*

Dr Douglas Davies, Professor in the Study of Religion, Department of Theology and Religion, University of Durham, UK: *Myths and Symbols*

Dr Theodore Gabriel, Honorary Research Fellow, Department of Religious Studies, University of Gloucestershire, UK: *Hinduism: Sacred Writings, Hinduism in the Modern World, Islam: Science, Art, and Culture*

Dr Malcolm Hamilton, Senior Lecturer, Department of Sociology, University of Reading, UK: *The Sociology of Religion*

Dr Paul Hedges, Senior Lecturer in Theology and Religious Studies: *Theological Approaches to the Study of Religion*

Dr Anna S. King, Reader in Theology and Religious Studies, University of Winchester, UK: *Hinduism: Beliefs*

Magdalen Lambkin, PhD, University of Glasgow, Scotland: Consultant, *Understanding Religion*

Dr Russell T. McCutcheon, Professor of Sociology of Religion, University of Alabama, USA: *What is Religion?*

Dr Christopher Partridge, Professor of Religious Studies, University of Lancaster, UK: *Phenomenology and the Study of Religion, Rapid Fact-finder*

Naren Patel: *I am a Hindu*

Dr Tinu Ruparell, Associate Professor, Department of Religious Studies, University of Calgary, Canada: *Hinduism: Philosophy*

Revd Angela Tilby, Diocesan Canon, Christ Church, Oxford, UK: *Rapid Fact-finder*

Dr Maya Warrier, Lecturer on Hinduism, University of Wales, Trinity St David, UK: *Hinduism: A Historical Overview, Worship and Festivals, Family and Society*

Dr Fraser N. Watts, Starbridge Lecturer in Theology and Natural Science, University of Cambridge, UK: *The Psychology of Religion*

Revd Dr John-David Yule, Incumbent of the United Benefice of Fen Drayton with Conington, Lolworth, and Swavesey, Cambridge, UK: *Rapid Fact-finder*

List of Maps

List of Time Charts

List of Festival Charts

List of Illustrations

Preface

This volume and five other titles in the *Brief Introductions* series are taken directly from the third edition of *Introduction to World Religions*, edited by Christopher Partridge and revised by Tim Dowley. Additional maps and images are included from *Atlas of World Religions*, edited by Tim Dowley. We recognized that smaller volumes focused on specific religious traditions might be especially helpful for use in corresponding religious studies courses. General readers who are eager to know and understand more about religious beliefs and practices will find this series to be an engaging and accessible way to explore the world's religions—one by one.

Other Books in the Series
A Brief Introduction to Buddhism
A Brief Introduction to Christianity
A Brief Introduction to Islam
A Brief Introduction to Jainism and Sikhism
A Brief Introduction to Judaism

PART I
UNDERSTANDING RELIGION

SUMMARY

Belief in something that exists beyond or outside our understanding – whether spirits, gods, or simply a particular order to the world – has been present at every stage in the development of human society, and has been a major factor in shaping much of that development. Unsurprisingly, many have devoted themselves to the study of religion, whether to understand a particular set of beliefs, or to explain why humans seem instinctively drawn to religion. While biologists, for example, may seek to understand what purpose religion served in our evolutionary descent, we are concerned here with the beliefs, rituals, and speculation about existence that we – with some reservation – call religion.

The question of what 'religion' actually is is more fraught than might be expected. Problems can arise when we try to define the boundaries between religion and philosophy when speculation about existence is involved, or between religion and politics when moral teaching or social structure are at issue. In particular, once we depart from looking at the traditions of the West, many contend that such apparently obvious distinctions should not be applied automatically.

While there have always been people interested in the religious traditions of others, such 'comparative' approaches are surprisingly new. Theology faculties are among the oldest in European universities, but, while the systematic internal exploration of a religion provides considerable insights, many scholars insisted that the examination of religions more generally should be conducted instead by objective observers. This phenomenological approach was central to the establishment of the study of religion as a discipline in its own right. Others, concerned with the nature of society, or the workings of the human mind, for example, were inevitably drawn to the study of religion to expand their respective areas. More recently, many have attempted to utilise the work of these disparate approaches. In particular, many now suggest that – because no student can ever be entirely objective – theological studies are valuable because of their ability to define a religion in its own terms: by engaging with this alongside other, more detached, approaches, a student may gain a more accurate view of a particular religion.

CHAPTER I

What Is Religion?

Although no one is certain of the word's origins, we know that 'religion' derives from Latin, and that languages influenced by Latin have equivalents to the English word 'religion'. In Germany, the systematic study of religion is known as *Religionswissenschaft*, and in France as *les sciences religieuses*. Although the ancient words to which we trace 'religion' have nothing to do with today's meanings — it may have come from the Latin word that meant to tie something tightly (*religare*) — it is today commonly used to refer to those beliefs, behaviours, and social institutions which have something to do with speculations on any, and all, of the following: the origin, end, and significance of the universe; what happens after death; the existence and wishes of powerful, non-human beings such as spirits, ancestors, angels, demons, and gods; and the manner in which all of this shapes human behaviour.

Because each of these makes reference to an invisible (that is, non-empirical) world that somehow lies outside of, or beyond, human history, the things we name as 'religious' are commonly thought to be opposed to those institutions which we label as 'political'. In the West today we generally operate under the assumption that, whereas religion is a matter of personal belief that can never be settled by rational debate, such things as politics are observable, public, and thus open to rational debate.

THE ESSENCE OF 'RELIGION'

Although this commonsense distinction between private and public, sentiment and action, is itself a historical development — it is around the seventeenth century that we first see evidence that words that once referred to one's behaviour, public standing, and social rank (such as piety and reverence) became sentimentalized as matters of private feeling — today the assumption that religion involves an inner core of belief that is somehow expressed publicly in ritual is so widespread that to question it appears counterintuitive. It is just this assumption that inspires a number of people who, collectively, we could term 'essentialists'. They are 'essentialists' because they maintain that 'religion' names the outward behaviours that are inspired by the inner thing they call 'faith'. Hence, one can imagine someone saying, 'I'm not religious, but I'm spiritual.' Implicit here is the assumption that the institutions associated with religions — hierarchies, regulations, rituals, and so on — are merely secondary and inessential; the important thing is the inner faith, the inner 'essence' of religion. Although the essence of religion – the thing without which someone is thought to be non-religious – is known by various names (faith, belief, the Sacred, the Holy, and so on), essentialists are in general agreement that the essence of religion is real and non-empirical (that is, it cannot itself be seen, heard, touched, and so on); it defies study and must be experienced first-hand.

THE FUNCTION OF 'RELIGION'

Apart from an approach that assumes an inner experience, which underlies religious behaviour, scholars have used the term 'religion' for what they consider to be curious areas of observable human behaviour which require an explanation. Such people form theories to account for why it is people think, for example, that an invisible part of their body, usually called 'the soul', outlives that body; that powerful beings control the universe; and that there is more to existence than what is observable. These theories are largely functionalist; that is, they seek to determine the social, psychological, or political role played by the things we refer to as 'religious'. Such functionalists include historically:

- Karl Marx (1818–83), whose work in political economy understood religion to be a pacifier that deadened oppressed people's sense of pain and alienation, while simultaneously preventing them from doing something about their lot in life, since ultimate responsibility was thought to reside in a being who existed outside history.

Karl Marx (1818–83).

- Émile Durkheim (1858–1917), whose sociology defined religious as sets of beliefs and practices to enable individuals who engaged in them to form a shared, social identity.
- Sigmund Freud (1856–1939), whose psychological studies prompted him to liken religious behaviour to the role that dreams play in helping people to vent antisocial anxieties in a manner that does not threaten their place within the group.

Although these classic approaches are all rather different, each can be understood as *functionalist* insomuch as religion names an institution that has a role to play in helping individuals and communities to reproduce themselves.

THE FAMILY RESEMBLANCE APPROACH

Apart from the *essentialist* way of defining religion (i.e. there is some non-empirical, core feature without which something is not religious) and the *functionalist* (i.e. that religions help to satisfy human needs), there is a third approach: the *family resemblance* definition. Associated with the philosophy of Ludwig Wittgenstein (1889–1951), a family resemblance approach assumes that nothing is defined by merely one essence or function. Rather, just as members of a family more or less share a series of traits, and just as all things we call 'games' more or less share a series of traits – none of which is distributed evenly across all members of those groups we call 'family' or 'games' – so all things – including religion – are defined insomuch as they more or less share a series of delimited traits. Ninian Smart (1927–2001), who identified seven dimensions of religion that are present in religious traditions with varying degrees of emphasis, is perhaps the best known proponent of this view.

'RELIGION' AS CLASSIFIER

Our conclusion is that the word 'religion' likely tells us more about the user of the word (i.e. the classifier) than it does about the thing being classified. For instance, a Freudian psychologist will not conclude that religion functions to oppress the masses, since the Freudian theory precludes coming up with this Marxist conclusion. On the other hand, a scholar who adopts Wittgenstein's approach will sooner or later come up with a case in which something seems to share some traits, but perhaps not enough to count as 'a religion'. If, say, soccer matches satisfy many of the criteria of a religion, what might not also be called religion if soccer is? And what does such a broad usage do to the specificity, and thus utility, of the word 'religion'? As for those who adopt an essentialist approach, it is likely no coincidence that only those institutions with which one agrees are thought to be expressions of some authentic inner experience, sentiment, or emotion, whilst the traditions of others are criticized as being shallow and derivative.

So what is religion? As with any other item in our lexicon, 'religion' is a historical artefact that different social actors use for different purposes: to classify certain parts of their social world in order to celebrate, degrade, or theorize about them. Whatever else it may or may not be, religion is at least an item of rhetoric that group members use to sort out their group identities.

RUSSELL T. MCCUTCHEON

CHAPTER 2

Phenomenology and the Study of Religion

There is a long history of curiosity and scholarship regarding the religions of other people. However, the study of religions is a relative newcomer to academia. Greatly indebted to the impressive work and influence of the German scholar Friedrich Max Müller (1823–1900), the first university professorships were established in the final quarter of the nineteenth century. By the second half of the twentieth century, the study of religion had emerged as an important field of academic enquiry. In a period of history during which the rationalism of the earlier part of the century saw a decline, and in which there was increased interest in particularly non-Christian spirituality, since 1945 there has been a growth in courses in the study of religion offered in academic institutions. Moreover, work done in other disciplines has increasingly converged with the work done by students of religion (see the discussion in this book of 'The Anthropology of Religion', 'The Psychology of Religion', 'The Sociology of Religion', and 'Critical Theory and Religion').

These factors, amongst others, have made it possible for the study of religion in most Western universities to pull away from its traditional place alongside the study of Christian theology and establish itself as an independent field of enquiry. Whereas earlier in the century the study of non-Christian faiths was usually undertaken in faculties of Christian theology, and studied as part of a theology degree, there was a move – particularly in the late 1960s and 1970s, when the term 'religious studies' became common currency – to establish separate departments of religious studies. Whilst in the United States and most of Western Europe religious studies tends to be considered a subject completely distinct from theology, in the United Kingdom it is quite common for universities to offer degree programmes in 'theology and religious studies', and the lines between the two disciplines are not so heavily drawn.

RELIGIONSPHÄNOMENOLOGIE

Phenomenology is distinct from other approaches to the study of religion in that it does not necessarily seek to understand the social nature of religion, it is not concerned to explore the psychological factors involved in religious belief, nor is it

During the Kumbh Mela festival in the holy city of Haridwar the Guru in his decorated chariot is escorted by holy men and pilgrims visiting the River Ganges, India.

especially interested in the historical development of religions. Rather its main concern has been descriptive, the classification of religious phenomena: objects, rituals, teachings, behaviours, and so on.

The term *Religionsphänomenologie* was first used by the Dutch scholar Pierre Daniel Chantepie de la Saussaye (1848–1920) in his work *Lehrbuch der Religions-geschichte* (1887), which simply documented religious phenomena. This might be described as 'descriptive' phenomenology, the aim being to gather information about the various religions and, as botanists might classify plants, identify varieties of particular religious phenomena. This classification of types of religious phenomena, the hallmark of the phenomenological method, can be seen in the works of scholars such as Ninian Smart (1927–2001) and Mircea Eliade (1907–86). Descriptive phenomenology of the late nineteenth and early twentieth centuries tended to lead to accounts of religious phenomena which, to continue with the analogy, read much the same as a botanical handbook. Various species were identified (higher religion, lower religion, prophetic religion, mystical religion, and so on) and particular religious beliefs and practices were then categorized, discussed, and compared.

As the study of religion progressed, phenomenology came to refer to a method which was more complex, and claimed rather more for itself, than Chantepie's mere cataloguing of facts. This later development in the discipline – which was due in part to the inspiration of the philosophy of Edmund Husserl (1859–1938) – recognized how easy it is for prior beliefs and interpretations unconsciously to influence one's thinking. Hence, scholars such as Gerardus van der Leeuw (1890–1950) stressed the need for phenomenological *epoché*: the 'bracketing' or shelving of the question about the ontological or objective status of the religious appearances to consciousness. Thus questions about the objective or independent truth of Kali, Allah, or the Holy Spirit are initially laid aside. The scholar seeks to suspend judgment about the beliefs of those he studies in order to gain greater objectivity and accuracy in understanding. Also central to phenomenology is the need for empathy (*Einfühlung*), which helps towards an understanding of the religion from within. Students of a religion seek to feel their way into the beliefs of others by empathizing with them. Along with this suspension of judgment and empathy, phenomenologists spoke of 'eidetic vision', the capacity of the observer to see beyond the particularities of a religion and to grasp its core essence and meaning. Whilst we often see only what we want, or expect, to see, eidetic vision is the ability to see a phenomenon without such distortions and limitations. Hence, later phenomenologists did not merely catalogue the facts of religious history, but by means of *epoché*, empathy, and eidetic vision sought to understand their meaning for the believer. Although phenomenologists are well aware that there will always be some distance between the believer's understandings of religious facts and those of the scholar, the aim of phenomenology is, as far as possible, to testify only to what has been observed. It aims to strip away all that would stand in the way of a neutral, judgment-free presentation of the facts.

THE IDEA OF THE HOLY

Some scholars have gone beyond this simple presentation of the facts and claimed more. A classic example is Rudolf Otto's (1869–1937) book *Das Heilige* (*The Idea of the Holy*, 1917). On the basis of his study of religions, Otto claimed that central to all religious expression is an a priori sense of 'the numinous' or 'the holy'. This, of course, necessarily goes beyond a simple presentation of the facts of religious history to the development of a particular philosophical interpretation of those facts. The central truth of all religion, claimed Otto, is a genuine feeling of awe or reverence in the believer, a sense of the 'uncanny' inspired by an encounter with the divine. Otto did more than simply relate facts about religion; he assumed the existence of the holy – accepting the truth of encounters with the supernatural.

> 'Numinous dread' or awe characterizes the so-called 'religion of primitive man', where it appears as 'daemonic dread.'
>
> Rudolf Otto, *The Idea of the Holy*

For some scholars, for example Ninian Smart, such an assumption is unacceptable in the study of religion. To compromise objectivity in this way, Smart argued, skews the scholar's research and findings. What the scholar ends up with is not an unbiased account of the facts of religion, but a personal *theology* of religion.

NEUTRALITY

Whilst Otto's type of phenomenology clearly displays a basic lack of objectivity, it is now generally recognized that this is a problem intrinsic to the study of religions. Although many contemporary religious studies scholars would want to defend the notion of *epoché* as an ideal to which one should aspire, there is a question as to whether this ideal involves a certain naivety. For example, the very process of selection and production of typologies assumes a level of interpretation. To select certain facts rather than others, and to present them with other facts as a particular type of religion, presupposes some interpretation. What facts we consider important and unimportant, interesting or uninteresting, will be shaped by certain ideas that we hold, whether religious or non-religious. To be an atheist does not in itself make the scholar more objective and neutral. Hence, the belief in detached objectivity, and the claim to be purely 'descriptive', are now considered to be naive. The important thing is that, as we engage in study, we recognize and critically evaluate our beliefs, our presuppositions, our biases, and how they might shape the way we understand a religion (see 'Critical Theory and Religion').

INSIDERS AND OUTSIDERS

Another important issue in contemporary religious studies is the 'insider/outsider' problem. To what extent can a non-believer ('an outsider') understand a faith in the way the believer (an 'insider') does? It is argued that outsiders, simply because they are outsiders, will never fully grasp the insider's experience; even people who experience the same event at the same time will, because of their contexts and personal histories, interpret that experience in different ways. However, some scholars have insisted there is a definite advantage to studying religion from the outside – sometimes referred to as the 'etic' perspective. Members of a religion may be conditioned by, or pressurized into accepting, a particular – and often narrow – understanding of their faith, whereas the outsider is in the scholarly position of not being influenced by such pressures and conditioning. Impartiality and disinterest allow greater objectivity.

There is undoubtedly value in scholarly detachment. However – while the scholar may have a greater knowledge of the history, texts, philosophy, structure, and social implications of a particular faith than the average believer – not to have experienced that faith from the inside is surely to have a rather large hole in the centre of one's understanding. Indeed, many insiders will insist that scholarly 'head-knowledge' is peripheral to the 'meaning' of their faith. Hence, others have noted the value of studying a religion as an 'insider', or at least relying heavily on the views of insiders – sometimes referred to as the 'emic' perspective.

RESPONSE THRESHOLD

In order to take account of the emic perspective, along with the emphasis on participant observation (see 'The Anthropology of Religion'), some have spoken of the 'response threshold' in religious studies. The crossing of the response threshold happens when insiders question the scholar's interpretations: etic interpretations are challenged by emic perspectives. An insider's perspective – which may conflict with scholarly interpretations – is felt to carry equal, if not more, weight. Wilfred Cantwell Smith (1916–2000) has even argued that no understanding of a faith is valid until it has been acknowledged by an insider. Religious studies are thus carried out in the context of a dialogue which takes seriously the views of the insider, in order to gain a deeper understanding of the insider's world view.

BEYOND PHENOMENOLOGY

In his book entitled *Beyond Phenomenology* (1999), Gavin Flood has argued that what is important in studying religions is 'not so much the distinction between the insider and the outsider, but between the critical and the non-critical'. Flood makes use of theories developed within the social sciences and humanities. With reference to the shift in contemporary theoretical discourse, which recognizes that all knowledge is tradition-specific and embodied within particular cultures (see 'Critical Theory and Religion'), Flood argues, firstly, that religions should not be abstracted and studied apart from the historical, political, cultural, linguistic, and social contexts. Secondly, he argues that scholars, who are likewise shaped by their own contexts, always bring conceptual baggage to the study of religion. Hence, whether because of the effect research has on the community being studied, or because the scholar's own prejudices, preconceptions, instincts, emotions, and personal characteristics significantly influence that research, the academic study of religion can never be neutral and purely objective. Flood thus argues for 'a rigorous metatheoretical discourse' in religious studies. Metatheory is the critical analysis of theory and practice, the aim of which is to 'unravel the underlying assumptions inherent in any research programme and to critically comment on them'.

Metatheory is thus important because it 'questions the contexts of inquiry, the nature of inquiry, and the kinds of interests represented in inquiry'. In so doing, it questions the idea of detached objectivity in the study of religion, and the notion that one can be a disinterested observer who is able to produce neutral descriptions of religious phenomena, free of evaluative judgments. Hence, scholars need always to engage critically with, and take account of, their own assumptions, prejudices, and presuppositions.

This means that holding a particular faith need not be a hindrance to the study of religion. One can, for example, be a Christian theologian and a good student of religion. But for scholars such as Flood, the important thing is not the faith or lack of it, but the awareness of, and the critical engagement with, one's assumptions: 'It is critique rather than faith that is all important.'

It is worth noting that recent work, mainly in France, sees new possibilities for the philosophy of religion through a turn to phenomenology. Much of this work has been done in response to the important French Jewish philosopher Emmanuel Levinas (1905–95). The names particularly associated with this turn are Jean-Luc Marion, Dominique Janicaud, Jean-Luc Chretien, Michel Henry, and Alain Badiou. Marion, for example, has written on the phenomenology of the gift in theology, Badiou has responded to Levinas arguing against his emphasis on the importance of 'the other', and Chretien has written on the phenomenology of prayer.

CHRISTOPHER PARTRIDGE

CHAPTER 3

The Anthropology of Religion

Anthropology approaches religion as an aspect of culture. Religious beliefs and practices are important because they are central to the ways in which we organize our social lives. They shape our understanding of our place in the world, and determine how we relate to one another and to the rest of the natural, and supernatural, order. The truth or falsity of religious beliefs, or the authenticity or moral worth of religious practices, are seldom an issue for anthropologists, whose main concern is to document what people think and do, rather than determine what they ought to believe, or how they should behave.

RELIGION AND SOCIAL STRUCTURE

An early observation in the anthropology of religion was the extent to which religion and social structure mirror one another. Both the French historian Fustel de Coulanges (1830–89), drawing on Classical sources, and the Scottish biblical scholar William Robertson Smith (1846–94), who studied Semitic religions, demonstrated this coincidence in form. For example, nomadic peoples such as the Bedouin conceive of God in terms

> *The belief in a supreme God or a single God is no mere philosophical speculation; it is a great practical idea.*
>
> Maurice Hocart

of a father, and use familial and pastoral imagery to describe their relationship with God. A settled, hierarchical society, by contrast, will depict God as a monarch to whom tribute is due, with imagery of servants and subjects honouring a supreme ruler. These early studies influenced the French sociologist Émile Durkheim (1858–1917), whose book *The Elementary Forms of the Religious Life* (1912) was foundational for later anthropological studies of religion. Rather than seeing religion as determining social structure, Durkheim argued that religion is a projection of society's highest values and goals. The realm of the sacred is separated from the profane world and made to seem both natural and obligatory. Through collective rituals people both reaffirm their belief in supernatural beings and reinforce their bonds with one another.

The totemism of Australian Aboriginals, which links human groups with particular forms of animal or other natural phenomena in relations of prohibition and prescription, was regarded by many nineteenth-century scholars as the earliest form of religion, and as such was of interest to both Durkheim and the anthropologist Edward Burnett Tylor

(1832–1917), who postulated an evolutionary movement from animism to polytheism and then monotheism. However, as evolutionary arguments are essentially unprovable, later work built not on these foundations, but on the more sociological insights of Durkheim and anthropologists such as Alfred Radcliffe-Brown (1881–1955) and Sir Edward Evan Evans-Pritchard (1902–73).

Evans-Pritchard sought to retain the historical perspective of his predecessors, while replacing speculation concerning origins with data based on first-hand observations and participation in the life of a people. His classic 1937 ethnography of witchcraft, oracles, and magic among the Azande in Central Africa demonstrated that beliefs which, from a Western perspective, appear irrational and unscientific – such as the existence of witches and magic – are perfectly logical, once one understands the ideational system on which a society is based.

SYMBOLISM

While Durkheim was avowedly atheist, some of the most influential anthropologists of the later twentieth century, including Evans-Pritchard, were or became practising Roman Catholics. This is true of Mary Douglas (1921–2007) and Victor Turner (1920–83), both of whom were particularly interested in the symbolic aspects of religion. They were influenced not only by Durkheim and Evans-Pritchard, but more particularly by Durkheim's gifted pupils Marcel Mauss (1872–1950) and Henri Hubert (1864–1925), who wrote on ceremonial exchange, sacrifice, and magic.

> Man is an animal suspended in webs of significance he himself has spun. I take culture to be those webs.
>
> Clifford Geertz, *The Interpretation of Cultures: Selected Essays* (New York, 1973)

In her influential collection of essays *Purity and Danger* (1966), Douglas looked at the ways in which the human body is used as a symbol system in which meanings are encoded. The body is seen as a microcosm of the powers and dangers attributed to society at large. Thus, a group that is concerned to maintain its social boundaries, such as members of the Brahman caste in India, pays great attention to notions of purity and pollution as they affect the individual body. In examining purity rules, Douglas was primarily concerned with systems of classification. In her study of the Hebrew purity rules in the book of Leviticus, for example, Douglas argued that dietary proscriptions were not the result of medical or hygiene concerns, but followed the logic of a system of classification that divided animals into clean and unclean species according to whether they conformed to certain rules – such as being cloven-hooved and chewing cud – or were anomalous, and therefore unclean and prohibited. Like Robertson Smith, Douglas observed that rituals can retain their form over many generations, notwithstanding changes in their interpretation, and that meaning is preserved in the form itself, as well as in explanations for a particular ritual action.

In the work of Mary Douglas we see a fruitful combination of the sociological and symbolist tradition of the Durkheimians and the structuralism of Claude Lévi-Strauss (1908–2009). Lévi-Strauss carried out some fieldwork in the Amazonian region of Brazil,

A BRIEF INTRODUCTION TO HINDUISM

but it is as a theoretician that he has been most influential, looking not at the meaning or semantics of social structure, but at its syntax or formal aspects. In his four-volume study of mythology (1970–81), he sought to demonstrate the universality of certain cultural themes, often expressed as binary oppositions, such as the transformation of food from raw to cooked, or the opposition between culture and nature. The structuralism of Lévi-Strauss both looks back to Russian formalism and the linguistics of the Swiss Ferdinand de Saussure (1857–1913), and forwards to more recent psychoanalytic studies of religion, both of which see themselves as belonging more to a scientific than to a humanist tradition.

RITUAL AND SYMBOL

On the symbolist and interpretive side, Victor Turner (1920–83) produced a series of sensitive, detailed studies of ritual and symbols, focusing on the processual nature of ritual and its theatrical, dramatic aspects, based on extensive fieldwork among the Ndembu of Zambia carried out in the 1950s. Clifford Geertz (1926–2006) was equally concerned with meaning and interpretation, and following a German-American tradition he looked more at culture than at social structure. Geertz saw religion as essentially that which gives meaning to human society, and religious symbols as codifying an ethos or world view. Their power lies in their ability both to reflect and to shape society.

Recently, important changes have stemmed from postmodernism and postcolonial thinking, globalization and multiculturalism. Anthropologists now often incorporate a critique of their own position and interests into their studies, and are no longer preoccupied exclusively with 'exotic' small-scale societies; for instance, there is a lot of research into global Pentecostalism and its local forms. The impact of new forms of media in the religious sphere has also become a significant area of study.

FIONA BOWIE

MYTHS AND SYMBOLS

One dimension of religions which has received particular attention by scholars has been that of myths and symbols. If we had just heard a moving piece of music, we would find it strange if someone asked us whether the music were true or false. Music, we might reply, is neither true nor false; to ask such a question is inappropriate. Most people know that music can, as it were, speak to them, even though no words are used.

As with music so with people. The question of what someone 'means' to you cannot fully be answered by saying that he is your husband or she is your wife, because there are always unspoken levels of intuition, feeling, and emotion built into relationships. The question of 'meaning' must always be seen to concern these dimensions, as well as the more obviously factual ones.

Myths

Myths take many forms, depending on the culture in which they are found. But their function is always that of pinpointing vital issues and values in the life of the society concerned. They often dramatize those profound issues of life and death, of how humanity came into being, and of what life means, of how we should conduct ourselves as a citizen or spouse, as a creature of God or as a farmer, and so on.

Myths are not scientific or sociological theories about these issues; they are the outcome of the way a nation or group has pondered the great questions. Their function is not merely to provide a theory of life that can be taken or left at will; they serve to compel a response from humanity. We might speak of myths as bridges between the intellect and emotion, between the mind and heart – and in this, myths are like music. They express an idea and trigger our response to it.

Sometimes myths form an extensive series, interlinking with each other and encompassing many aspects of life, as has been shown for the Dogon people of the River Niger in West Africa. On the other hand, they may serve merely as partial accounts of problems, such as the hatred between people and snakes, or the reason for the particular shape of a mountain.

One problem in our understanding of myths lies in the fact that the so-called Western religions – Judaism, Christianity, and Islam – are strongly concerned with history. They have founders, and see their history as God's own doing. This strong emphasis upon actual events differs from the Eastern approaches to religion, which emphasize the consciousness of the individual. Believing in the cyclical nature of time, Hinduism and Buddhism possess a different approach to history, and hence also to science.

In the West, the search for facts in science is like the search for facts in history, but both these endeavours differ from the search for religious experience in the present. In the West, history and science have come to function as a framework within which religious experiences are found and interpreted, one consequence of which is that myths are often no longer appreciated for their power to evoke human responses to religious ideas.

The eminent historian of religion Mircea Eliade (1907–86) sought to restore this missing sense of the sacred by helping people to understand the true nature of myths. The secularized Westerner has lost the sense of the sacred, and is trying to compensate, as Eliade saw it, by means of science fiction, supernatural literature, and films. One may, of course, keep a firm sense of history and science without seeking to destroy the mythical appreciation of ideas and beliefs.

Symbols

Religious symbols help believers to understand their faith in quite profound ways. Like myths, they serve to unite the intellect and the emotions. Symbols also integrate the social and personal dimensions of religion, enabling individuals to share certain commonly held beliefs expressed by symbols, while also giving freedom to read private meaning into them.

We live the whole of our life in a world of symbols. The daily smiles and grimaces, handshakes and greetings, as well as the more readily acknowledged status symbols of large cars or houses – all these communicate messages about ourselves to others.

To clarify the meaning of symbols, it will help if we distinguish between the terms 'symbol' and 'sign'. There is a certain arbitrariness about signs, so that the word 'table', which signifies an object of furniture with a flat top supported on legs, could be swapped for another sound without any difficulty. Thus the Germans call it *tisch* and the Welsh *bwrdd*.

A symbol, by contrast, is more intimately involved in that to which it refers. It participates in what it symbolizes, and cannot easily be swapped for another symbol. Nor can it be explained in words and still carry the same power. For example, a kiss is a symbol of affection and love; it not only signifies these feelings in some abstract way; it actually demonstrates them. In this sense a symbol can be a thought in action.

Religious symbols share these general characteristics, but are often even more intensely powerful, because they enshrine and express the highest values and relationships of life. The cross of Christ, the sacred books of Muslims and Sikhs, the sacred cow of Hindus, or the silent, seated Buddha – all these command the allegiance of millions of religious men and women. If such symbols are attacked or desecrated, an intense reaction is felt by the faithful, which shows us how deeply symbols are embedded in the emotional life of believers.

The power of symbols lies in this ability to unite fellow-believers into a community. It provides a focal point of faith and action, while also making possible a degree of personal understanding which those outside may not share.

In many societies the shared aspect of symbols is important as a unifying principle of life. Blood, for example, may be symbolic of life, strength, parenthood, or of the family and kinship group itself. In Christianity it expresses life poured out in death, the self-sacrificial love of Christ who died for human sin. It may even be true that the colour red can so easily serve as a symbol of

The cross is the central symbol of Christianity.

danger because of its deeper biological association with life and death.

Symbols serve as triggers of commitment in religions. They enshrine the teachings and express them in a tangible way. So the sacraments of baptism and the Lord's Supper in Christianity bring the believer into a practical relationship with otherwise abstract ideas, such as repentance and forgiveness. People can hardly live without symbols because they always need something to motivate life; it is as though abstract ideas need to be set within a symbol before individuals can be impelled to act upon them. When any attempt is made to turn symbols into bare statements of truth, this vital trigger of the emotions can easily be lost.

Douglas Davies

CHAPTER 4

The Sociology of Religion

The sociological study of religion has its roots in the seventeenth- and eighteenth-century Enlightenment, when a number of influential thinkers sought not only to question religious belief, but also to understand it as a natural phenomenon, a human product rather than the result of divine revelation or revealed truth. While contemporary sociology of religion has largely abandoned the overtly critical stance of early theoretical approaches to the truth claims of religion, the discipline retains the essential principle that an understanding of religion must acknowledge that it is, to some degree at least, socially constructed, and that social processes are fundamentally involved in the emergence, development, and dissemination of religious beliefs and practices.

METHODOLOGICAL AGNOSTICISM

While some sociologists consider that some religious beliefs are false, and that recognition of this is crucial to a sociological understanding of them, the dominant position in the sociology of religion today is that of 'methodological agnosticism'. This method states that it is neither possible, nor necessary, to decide whether beliefs are true or false in order to study them sociologically. Theology and philosophy of religion, not sociology, discuss questions of religious truth. The conditions which promote the acceptance or rejection of religious beliefs and practices, which govern their dissemination and the impact they have on behaviour and on society, can all be investigated without prior determination of their truth or falsity.

ROOTS IN INDIVIDUAL NEEDS

Theoretical approaches in the sociology of religion can usefully – if a little crudely – be divided into those which perceive the roots of religion to lie in individual needs and propensities, and those which perceive its roots to lie in social processes and to stem from the characteristics of society and social groups. The former may be further divided into those which emphasize cognitive processes – intellectualism – and those which emphasize various feelings and emotions – emotionalism.

In the nineteenth century, intellectualist theorists such as Auguste Comte (1798–1857), Edward Burnett Tylor (1832–1917), James G. Frazer (1854–1941), and Herbert Spencer (1820–1903) analyzed religious belief as essentially a pre-scientific attempt to understand the world and human experience, which would increasingly be supplanted by sound scientific knowledge. The future would thus be entirely secular, with no place for religion.

Emotionalist theorists, such as Robert Ranulph Marett (1866–1943), Bronislaw Malinowski (1884–1942), and Sigmund Freud (1856–1939), saw religions as stemming from human emotions such as fear, uncertainty, ambivalence, and awe. They were not attempts to explain and understand, but to cope with intense emotional experience.

ROOTS IN SOCIAL PROCESSES

The most influential sociological approaches that consider the roots of religion lie in society and social processes, not in the individual, are those of Karl Marx (1818–83) and Émile Durkheim (1858–1917).

For Marx, religion was both a form of ideology supported by ruling classes in order to control the masses, and at the same time an expression of protest against such oppression – 'the sigh of the oppressed creature'. As a protest, however, it changed nothing, promoting only resignation, and promising resolution of problems in the afterlife. Religion is 'the opium of the people', in the sense that it dulls the pain of the oppressed and thereby stops them from revolting. Hence, the oppressed turn to religion to help them get through life; the ruling classes promote it to keep them in check. It will simply disappear when the social conditions that cause it are removed.

> *Religion is the sigh of the oppressed creature and the opium of the people.*
>
> Karl Marx, A Contribution to the Critique of Hegel's Philosophy of Right (Deutsch-Französische Jahrbücher, 1844).

Durkheim saw religion as an essential, integrating social force, which fulfilled basic functions in society. It was the expression of human subordination, not to a ruling class, as Marx had argued, but rather to the requirements of society itself, and to social pressures which overrule individual preferences. In his famous work *The Elementary Forms of the Religious Life* (1912), Durkheim argued that 'Religion is society worshipping itself.' God may not exist, but society does; rather than God exerting pressure on the individual to conform, society itself exerts the pressure. Individuals, who do not understand the nature of society and social groups, use the language of religion to explain the social forces they experience. Although people misinterpret social forces as religious forces, what they experience is real. Moreover, for Durkheim, religion fulfils a positive role, in that it binds society together as a moral community.

MAX WEBER AND MEANING THEORY

Later theoretical approaches in the sociology of religion have all drawn extensively on this earlier work, attempting to synthesize its insights into more nuanced approaches, in which the various strands of intellectual, emotional, and social factors are woven together. A notable example is the work of Max Weber (1864–1920), probably the most significant contributor to the sociology of religion to this day. His work included one of the best-known treatises in the sub-discipline, *The Protestant Ethic and the Spirit of Capitalism* (1904–05), and three major studies of world religions.

Weber's approach to religion was the forerunner of what has become known as 'meaning theory', which emphasizes the way in which religion gives meaning to human life and society, in the face of apparently arbitrary suffering and injustice. Religion offers explanation and justification of good and of bad fortune, by locating them within a broader picture of a reality which may go beyond the world of immediate everyday perception, thereby helping to make sense of what always threatens to appear senseless. So those who suffer undeservedly in this life may have offended in a previous one; or they will receive their just deserts in the next life, or in heaven. Those who prosper through wickedness will ultimately be judged and duly punished.

RATIONAL CHOICE THEORY

The most recent, general theoretical approach in the sociology of religion, which synthesizes many previous insights, is that of 'rational choice theory'. Drawing upon economic theory, this treats religions as rival products offered in a market by religious organizations – which are compared to commercial firms – and leaders, to consumers, who choose by assessing which best meets their needs, which is most reliable, and so on. This approach promises to provide many insights. However, it has been subjected to trenchant criticism by those who question whether religion can be treated as something chosen in the way that products such as cars or soap-powders are chosen, rather than something into which people are socialized, and which forms an important part of their identity that cannot easily be set aside or changed. Furthermore, if religious beliefs are a matter of preference and convenience, why do their followers accept the uncongenial demands and constraints they usually impose, and the threat of punishments for failure to comply?

SECULARIZATION AND NEW MOVEMENTS

The sociology of religion was for many decades regarded as an insignificant branch of sociology. This situation has changed in recent years, especially in the USA. Substantive empirical inquiry has been dominated by two areas: secularization and religious sects, cults, and movements. It had been widely assumed that religion was declining in modern industrial societies and losing its social significance – the secularization thesis. This has

been questioned and found by many — especially rational choice theorists — to be wanting. The result has been intense

Hare Krishna Festival of Chariots in Trafalgar Square, London. Hare Krishna is one of many New Religious Movements.

debate. The dominant position now, though not unchallenged, is that the secularization thesis was a myth.

Central to this debate is the claim that — while religion in its traditional forms may be declining in some modern, Western industrial societies — it is not declining in all of them, the USA being a notable exception; and that novel forms of religion are continuously emerging to meet inherent spiritual needs. Some new forms are clearly religious in character. Others, it is claimed, are quite unlike religion as commonly understood, and include alternative and complementary forms of healing, psychotherapies, techniques for the development of human potential, deep ecology, holistic spirituality, New Age, the cult of celebrity, nationalist movements, and even sport. Whether such things can be considered forms of religion depends upon how religion is defined, a matter much disputed.

A second crucial element in the secularization debate is the rise of a diversity of sects and cults – the New Religious Movements – which have proliferated since the 1960s and 1970s. For the anti-secularization – or 'sacralization' – theorists, this flourishing of novel religiosity gives the lie to the thesis; while for pro-secularization theorists, such movements fall far short of making up for the decline of mainstream churches and denominations. Whatever their significance for the secularization thesis, the New Religious Movements – and sects and cults in general – have fascinated sociologists, whose extensive studies of them form a major part of the subject.

Heavy concentration on New Religious Movements has been balanced more recently by studies of more mainstream religious churches and communities, and by studies of the religious life of ethnic minorities and immigrant communities, among whom religion is often particularly significant and an important element of identity. Added to the interest in new forms of religion and quasi-religion, such studies make the contemporary sociology of religion more diverse and varied than ever.

MALCOLM HAMILTON

CHAPTER 5

The Psychology of Religion

Three key figures dominate the psychology of religion that we have inherited from the pre-World War II period: William James, Sigmund Freud, and C. G. Jung.

WILLIAM JAMES (1842–1910)

The undoubted masterpiece of the early days of the psychology of religion is the classic *Varieties of Religious Experience*, written by William James at the end of the nineteenth century. James assembled an interesting compendium of personal reports of religious experience, and embedded them in a rich and subtle framework of analysis. He thought religious experience was essentially an individual matter, the foundation on which religious doctrine and church life were built. However, from the outset his critics argued that religious experience is in fact interpreted within the framework of inherited religious teaching and shaped by the life of the institution. James hoped to put religion on a scientific basis, through the scientific study of religious experience, although he was unable to make a really convincing case for accepting religious experience at face value. Despite these issues, even his critics have never doubted the quality of his work, which is as hotly debated now as when it was first written.

SIGMUND FREUD (1856–1939)

Another important figure in the development of the psychology of religion was Sigmund Freud, although his approach was very different from that of James. Freud built his general theories upon what patients told him during their psychoanalysis, although he reported only one case study in which religion played a central part. This was the so-called 'wolf man', in whom religion and obsessionality were intertwined, which led Freud to suggest that religion was a universal form of obsessional neurosis. In fact, Freud's psychology of religion was hardly based on data at all; it was a blend of general psychoanalytic theory and his own personal hostility to religion. He wrote several books about religion, each taking a different approach. The clearest is *The Future of an Illusion*, which claims that religion is merely 'illusion', which for him is a technical term meaning wish-fulfilment.

Freud's successors have argued that what he called illusion, including religion, is in fact much more valuable than he realized to people in helping them to adjust to life.

C. G. JUNG (1875–1961)

Freud's approach to religion was continued in modified form by Carl Gustav Jung. Whereas Freud had been a harsh critic of religion, Jung was favourably disposed to it. However, his approach to religion was so idiosyncratic that many have found him an uncomfortable friend. Jung made a distinction between the ego – the centre of conscious life – and the self – the whole personality that people can potentially become. For Jung, the self is the image of God in the psyche, and the process of 'individuation' – that is, development from

Sigmund Freud (1856–1939).

Religious ideas … are illusions, fulfilments of the oldest, strongest, and most urgent wishes of mankind.

Sigmund Freud, *The Future of an Illusion* (London: Hogarth, 1962).

ego-centred life to self-centred life – is in some ways analogous to religious salvation. Jung was evasive about the question of whether there was a god beyond the psyche, and usually said it was not a question for him as a psychologist. Jung took more interest in the significance of Christian doctrine than most psychologists and, for example, wrote long essays on the Mass and on the Trinity.

THE PSYCHOLOGY OF RELIGION TODAY

The psychology of religion went relatively quiet around the middle of the twentieth century, but has been reviving in recent decades. It has become more explicitly scientific, and most psychological research on religion now uses quantitative methods. There are currently no big psychological theories of religion, but important insights have been obtained about various specific aspects of religion. The following examples give a flavour of current work.

- *Individual differences.* One useful distinction has been between 'intrinsic' religious people – those for whom religion is the dominant motivation in their lives – and 'extrinsic' religious people – those for whom religion meets other needs. Intrinsics and extrinsics differ from one another in many ways. For example, it has been suggested that intrinsically religious people show less social prejudice than non-religious people, whereas extrinsically religious people show more.

- *Religious development.* Children's understanding of religion follows a predictable path, moving from the concrete to the abstract. However, acquiring a better intellectual understanding of religion is not necessarily accompanied by a more spiritual experience. In fact, spiritual experience may actually decline as children grow up. There have been attempts to extend a development approach to religion into adulthood. For example, James Fowler developed a general theory of 'faith development'. Although this has identified different approaches to faith in adults, it is not clear that higher levels of faith necessarily follow the earlier ones, nor that they are superior.
- *Mental health.* Despite Freud's view that religion is a form of neurosis, scientific research has shown that there is often a positive correlation between religion and health, especially mental health. It is most likely that religion actually helps to improve people's mental health, although this is hard to prove conclusively. Religion probably helps by providing a framework of meaning and a supportive community, both of which enable people to cope better with stressful experiences.
- *Conservative and charismatic Christianity.* There has been much interest in both fundamentalism and charismatic religion. One key feature of fundamentalism is the 'black and white' mindset that maintains a sharp dichotomy between truth and falsehood, and between insiders and outsiders. The charismatic phenomenon that has attracted most research interest is speaking in tongues. It seems very unlikely that this is an actual language; it is probably more a form of ecstatic utterance. One line of research has explored the social context in which people learn to speak in tongues, and another the unusual state of consciousness in which people surrender voluntary control of their speech.

Although psychology has generally taken a detached, scientific view of religion, there are other points of contact. One is the incorporation of psychological methods into the Christian church's pastoral care, begun by Freud's Lutheran pastor friend, Oskar Pfister (1873–1956). Another is the dialogue between religious and psychological world-views, an aspect of the more general dialogue between science and religion. Some psychologists consider that humans are 'nothing but' the product of their evolution or their nervous systems, whereas religious faith emphasizes their importance in the purposes of God.

FRASER WATTS

CHAPTER 6

Theological Approaches to the Study of Religion

During the development of the study of religion as a new discipline in the twentieth century, the pioneers of the field were often at pains to stress that what they did was different from theology. As such, it might be asked whether a theological approach even belongs within the study of religion. Many scholars today, who emphasize it as a scientific or historical discipline, distance themselves from any notion that theology, in any form, has a place within the study of religion. For others, the relationship is more ambiguous, while some scholars even argue that theological approaches are essential to understanding, and so truly studying, religion.

WHAT DO WE MEAN BY 'THEOLOGY'?

It is best to start by defining what we mean by 'theology' in relation to the study of religion. We will begin with some negatives. First, it does not mean a confessional approach, where the teachings of one school, tradition, or sect within a religion are taught as the true, or correct, understanding of that religion. Second, theology does not imply that there is any need for a belief, or faith content, within the person studying in that idiom. It is not, therefore, under the classic definition of the medieval Christian Anselm of Canterbury (1033–1109), an act of 'faith seeking understanding'.

We come now to the positives. First, it is about understanding the internal terms within which a religion will seek to explain itself, its teachings, and its formulations. We must be clear here that 'theology' is used loosely, because while it makes sense as a Christian term — literally it is the study of God — and can be fairly clearly applied to other theistic traditions, it is also used elsewhere to talk about broadly philosophical traditions related to transcendence. Accordingly, people use the term 'Buddhist theology' — although others question whether this usage is appropriate, but space does not permit us to engage in such disputes here. Second, it means engaging with empathy with questions of meaning as they would make sense within the religious worldview, and so goes beyond reasoning and relates to a way of life. Here, we see clear resonances with phenomenological approaches, where we seek to understand a religion on its own terms.

Indeed, without a theological viewpoint, it can be argued that the study of religions fails, because on the one hand it is

Anselm of Canterbury (1033–1109).

either simply reductionist, that is to say it explains via some chosen system why the religion exists, what it does, and what it means — as tends to be the case with some parts of the sociology or psychology of religion. Or, on the other hand, it becomes merely descriptive, telling us what rituals are performed, what the ethics are, what the teachings are, how it is lived out, and so on — a simply phenomenological approach. A theological approach looks into the religion, and seeks to understand what it means to believers within its own terms, and how that system works as a rational worldview to those within it.

INSIDER AND OUTSIDER

Two important pairs of distinctions are useful to consider how theological approaches are applied. The first, developed by the anthropologist Kenneth Pike (1912–2000), and often applied to religion, concerns what are called 'emic' and 'etic' approaches. An emic approach attempts to explain things within the cultural world of the believer. An etic approach is the way an external observer would try and make sense of the behaviours and beliefs of a society or group in some form of scientific sense. Within anthropology, these basic distinctions are seen as part of the tools of the trade. Unless she enters into the thought-world of a group, culture, and society, the anthropologist will remain forever exterior, and will not understand what things mean to those in that group. Moreover, emic understandings can help inspire etic description, and assess its appropriateness. Clearly, in the study of religion, this originally anthropological distinction suggests that an emic, or theological, approach is justified.

Our second pair of distinctions is the notion of 'Insider' and 'Outsider' perspectives. These are, respectively, concepts from somebody who is a believer (an Insider), and a non-believer, that is, the scholar (an Outsider). This differs from the emic/etic distinction, because they are always perspectives of the Outsider: the scholar. As such, an emic theological approach is different from the confessional theology of an Insider. However, this distinction is often blurred. Field anthropologists speak of spending so much time within the group or society they study that they often almost become part of that group, and part of good fieldwork is about entering the life world of those studied. This applies equally to scholars of religion, especially those engaged in fieldwork.

Another issue is that scholars may be believers within a religion, and so may inhabit both Insider and Outsider worlds. This raises many interesting questions, but here we will note simply that the notion of the detached, impartial, and objective scholar is increasingly questioned. Issues raised by critical theory have suggested that every standpoint will always have a bias, and some have argued further – notably the Hindu scholar, Gavin Flood – that a religious point of view, if openly acknowledged, can form part of the broader study of religions. Moreover, religious groups are often affected by what scholars of religion say about them. Therefore, Insider worldviews and Outsider descriptions – etic or emic – become intertwined in a dance that affects each other. As such, the question of how a theological approach fits into, or works within, religious studies is far from simple.

ALWAYS 'TAINTED'?

Scholars such as Timothy Fitzgerald, Tomoko Masuzawa, and Tala Asad have argued that the supposedly secular study of religion has always been 'tainted', because it developed in a world where Christianity dominated – often with a particular kind of liberal theology – so that no study of religion is entirely free from theology. Certainly, some foundational figures, such as Mircea Eliade, had a religious worldview, and a lot of mid-twentieth century work developing the phenomenology of religion, or comparative religion, made assumptions about a religious realm that underlay all traditions. However, it is arguable whether all scholars of religion then and since are affected in this way, while a case can be made that it was not solely Christian assumptions that affected the study of religion, but that such assumptions were shaped by the encounter with various religious traditions. As such, while we must be suspicious of some categories within the study of religion, we do not need to assume that everything has a Christian basis. Indeed, Frank Whaling argues we must also not forget that many religions have a lot to say about other religions, and this leads into theorizing on comparative religion, comparative theology, and the theology of religions within a confessional standpoint which is not entirely separate from understanding a religion and its worldview.

The relationship of the study of religions and theology varies in different countries. For instance, in Germany the two tend to be starkly polarized, with theology departments being — at least traditionally — strictly confessional, normally Roman Catholic or Protestant, and the study of religions — understood as a primarily reductionist secular discipline — is always separate from theology. In the UK, the ancient universities started to admit non-Anglican Christian denominations from the nineteenth century, and so lost their confessional stance, with seminaries for training priests becoming separate or linked institutions. For this reason, it was easier to start teaching theology from a generic standpoint, which could integrate other religions as part of the curriculum, and so there are many combined departments for theology and the study of religion. The USA tends to have a more separate system, although there are places where an active study of religion discipline exists within a theology department. Obviously, such regional differences affect the way a theological approach to the study of religion is accepted or understood.

PAUL HEDGES

CHAPTER 7

Critical Theory and Religion

Our knowledge of 'religion' is always politically shaped, and never an innocent or a neutral activity. Knowledge about religion can always be questioned, and scholars of religion are finding that 'religion', and talk about 'religion', is involved with questions of power. Critical theory questions knowledge about 'religion', and reveals the social and political nature of such ideas.

DEFINING CRITICAL THEORY

Critical theory arises from a long tradition in Western thought which has questioned the truth and certainty of knowledge. It carries forward the work of the 'three great masters of suspicion', Karl Marx (1818–83), Friedrich Nietzsche (1844–1900), and Sigmund Freud (1856–1939). Following Marx, critical theory is aware that all knowledge is linked to economic and political ideology; following Nietzsche, it understands that all knowledge is linked to the 'will to power'; and following Freud, it understands that all knowledge is linked to things outside our awareness (the unconscious). The ideas of these three great thinkers influence, and are carried forward in, the work of critical theory. All three started to question the view that knowledge was neutral and rational.

There are two basic understandings of 'critical theory', a strict definition and a loose definition. The former relates to the Frankfurt School of Critical Theory, an important group of German intellectuals who tried to think about society according to the ideas of Marx and Freud.

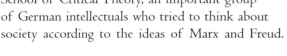

Friedrich Nietzsche (1844–1900).

They included Theodor Adorno (1903–69) and Max Horkheimer (1895–1973), who jointly published *Dialectic of Enlightenment*, a seminal work in which they questioned Western rational thought since the Enlightenment. What did it say about the potential of human knowledge if it could lead to the ideology of Nazi Germany and the horrors of the Holocaust? Culture was understood to be formed by propagandist manipulation.

The loose definition incorporates a wider range of critical theories, which emerged – largely in France – after the student riots of 1968 in Paris. This date is a watershed in modern Western intellectual history because it reflects, among many things, a shift in the thinking about state power and the control of ideas. It was an event that brought the questions of 'power' and 'politics' to the question of knowledge and truth.

POST-STRUCTURALISM

The critical thinking that emerged in 1968 in France is known as 'post-structuralism' because it comes after an intellectual movement known as 'structuralism'. Structuralism held that one could identify a given number of structures in myth, language, and the world. Post-structuralists argued that these structures were not 'given' in the fabric of the world, but created by different societies at different points of history and in different cultures. Michel Foucault (1926–84) examined the historical nature of ideas, showing that the ways we think about the world are related to political institutions and regimes of power. Jacques Derrida (1930–2004) showed that our ways of representing the world in texts holds hidden contradictions and tensions, because language is unstable and built upon assertions of power, not truth. The instability of language refers to the discovery that the meaning of words in a dictionary simply means other words, rather than something indisputable and fixed in the world, and that meanings are simply asserted or agreed, rather than having a strong foundation given for all time. These two prominent thinkers brought knowledge under question, and enabled scholars of religion to uncover how what is and what is not classified as 'religion' can benefit certain groups of people within society.

Critical theory is thus not an abstract and disengaged way of thinking, but an active ethical responsibility for the world and the way we think about the world. It shows the link between ideas and political practices.

> *Religion is a political force.*
>
> Michel Foucault

THE END OF PHENOMENOLOGY

Before critical theory, the study of religion often consisted of representing different religious traditions, and understanding them according to their rituals, beliefs, and practices. This is known as 'the phenomenology of religion', and is arguably still dominant in school and university programmes of study. Such an approach assumed that knowledge is neutral, and that different issues can be presented without too much difficulty. It was also assumed by many scholars that one does not need a 'theory' or 'theoretical position' –

a way of understanding knowledge and the world – to represent a religious tradition or a set of ideas. There was an assumption that language neutrally represented the external world according to a direct correspondence between the subject in representation (words) and the object in the external world (things) – in this case 'religious' things. However, knowledge and the categories used to represent the world and religion are now seen to be carrying hidden assumptions, with implications for gender, society, politics, colonial history, race, and ethnicity. All knowledge is now seen as reflecting a particular viewpoint or bias about the world; the production and acquisition of knowledge is never neutral. Hence, after critical theory, there is no neutral presentation of ideas about religion.

Critical theory is a way of thinking about how our dominant conceptions of religion come to be dominant or hegemonic. It seeks to identify the hidden positions within our knowledge, and to recognize that all ideas about religion hold a theoretical position about knowledge, even if that position is denied or not apparent. Critical theory offers a way of exploring 'religion' through a set of critical questions about the world and the ideas under discussion. It is not limited to the study of religion, but applies to all ways of thinking about the world, and even questions the boundary between different disciplines of knowledge. Critical theory is not a sub-discipline of religious studies – like the sociology, anthropology, or psychology of religion – but cuts across all these areas and questions all types of knowledge.

Critical theory questions the very idea of 'religion' as a Western – even Christian – category that assumes that belief is more important than how people live, which in turn is used to make assumptions about what people outside Christianity believe. This is seen as a distortion of other cultures. To correct such a view, critical theory considers traditions and cultures outside the bias of such an idea, which assumes there is something special and distinctive we can call 'religion' or 'religious'. For example, scholars question the Christian missionary interpretation of other cultures, and ask whether Hinduism is a 'religion' or the culture of South Asia. In turn, we may question whether Western capitalism is a culture or a religion. Critical theory draws attention to how knowledge is related to political ideas, and questions the domination of Western ideas (particularly European-American ideas) over other ways of seeing the world in different cultures and periods of history. It explores the way ideas powerfully rule the world and the 'truth' people have about the world.

RELIGION, POWER, AND CULTURE

Critical theory shows that the ways we think about religion are bound up in questions of power. Religious studies is now involved in exploring how the history and abuses of colonialism influenced the emergence of religion as an idea; how state power, political regimes, and the globalized world of capitalism affect this process; and how the mass media alter what we mean by religion, and uncover those activities and groups within society not recognized as religious. Critical theory exposes the abuses of power in history, and examines who benefits from thinking about the world in certain ways. It identifies those who are marginalized and unable to speak for themselves.

By examining race, gender, sexuality, and economic wealth one can see how ideas about religion often support those in power, usually the ruling educated elite of white, Western men. Thinking and writing about ideas from the position of the exploited radically changes the subject and the writing of history. Such a process questions, for example, the narrative of Christian history from its Roman-European bias, and examines Christianity through its African – particularly Ethiopian – traditions, highlighting the importance of Augustine as an African. It explores the involvement of Buddhist monks in political activism, and uncovers how the Western media distort the understanding of Islam. Critical theory also identifies ways of life outside the mainstream traditions, and explores the indigenous or local traditions around the world, which are suppressed by multinational business interests for land and oil.

Orthodox priests at a Christian festival at Timket, Ethiopia.

Critical theory questions the boundary between religion and culture, and argues that what people do – rather than what they believe – is more important in understanding. The distinction between the religious and the secular is seen as an ideological or political tool. According to this view, the category of 'religion' can be applied to all cultural activities, such as football, shopping, fashion, club-culture, and film. The historical roots of social institutions – such as government, schools, hospitals, and law – are shown to carry ideas that can be classified as religious, even if they are not transparent. Critical theory radically alters the understanding of religion and shows the importance of the idea to world history. After critical theory, the study of religion becomes a political activity, an account of how powerful organizations in different parts of the world shape the way we understand and classify the world.

JEREMY CARRETTE

CHAPTER 8

Ritual and Performance

Like myths and symbols, ritual and performance is an area that has particularly interested religious studies scholars. Ritual is patterned, formal, symbolic action. Religious ritual is usually seen as having reference to divine or transcendent beings, or perhaps ancestors, whom the participants invoke, propitiate, feed – through offering or sacrifice – worship, or otherwise communicate with. Rituals attempt to enact and deal with the central dilemmas of human existence: continuity and stability, growth and fertility, morality and immortality or transcendence. They have the potential to transform people and situations, creating a fierce warrior or docile wife, a loving servant or imperious tyrant. The ambiguity of ritual symbols, and the invocation of supernatural power, magnifies and disguises human needs and emotions. Because rituals are sometimes performed in terrifying circumstances – as in certain initiation rituals – the messages they carry act at a psycho-biological level that includes, but also exceeds, the rational mind. Symbols and sacred objects are manipulated within ritual to enhance performance and communicate ideological messages concerning the nature of the individual, society, and cosmos. Rituals are fundamental to human culture, and can be used to control, subvert, stabilize, enhance, or terrorize individuals and groups. Studying them gives us a key to an understanding and interpretation of culture.

Anthropologists and religious studies scholars sometimes look at rituals in terms of what they do. For instance, Catherine Bell (b. 1953) distinguishes between:
- rites of passage or 'life crisis' rituals
- calendrical rituals and commemorative rites
- rites of exchange or communication
- rites of affliction
- rites of feasting, fasting, festivals
- political rituals

Another approach is to focus on their explanatory value. Mircea Eliade (1907–86) was interested in ritual as a re-enactment of a primal, cosmogonic myth, bringing the past continually into the present. Robin Horton emphasizes the reality of the religious beliefs behind ritual actions. Using the Kalabari of Nigeria as an example, he insists that religious rituals have the power to move and transform participants because they express beliefs that have meaning and coherence for their adherents. Taking a lead from Durkheim (1858–1917), other scholars claim that rituals are effective because they make statements about social phenomena. Maurice Bloch, writing about circumcision rituals in Madagascar, makes the interesting observation that because a ritual is not fully a statement and not fully an action it allows its message to be simultaneously communicated and disguised. In some cases ritual symbols may be full of resonance, as Victor Turner demonstrated for Ndembu heali ng, chiefly installation, and initiation rituals in Central Africa. In other cases the performance of the ritual itself may be what matters, the content or symbolism having become redundant or forgotten over time, as Fritz Staal has argued for Vedic rituals in India.

> *No experience is too lowly to be taken up in ritual and given a lofty meaning.*
>
> Mary Douglas

PATTERNS IN RITUAL

A key figure in the study of ritual is Arnold van Gennep (1873–1957), who discerned an underlying patterning beneath a wide range of rituals. Whether we look at seasonal festivals such as Christmas, midsummer, or harvest, or 'life crisis' rituals that mark a change in status from one stage of life to another, such as birth, puberty, marriage, or mortuary rituals, we see beneath them all the threefold pattern of separation, transition, and reintegration. Van Gennep also noted that there is generally a physical passage in ritual as well as a social movement, and that the first time a ritual is celebrated it is usually more elaborate than on subsequent occasions, as it bears the weight of change of status.

Victor Turner took up van Gennep's schema, emphasizing the movement from social structure to an anti-structural position in the middle, liminal, stage of a rite of passage. In the middle stage, initiands often share certain characteristics. There is a levelling process – they may be stripped, or dressed in such a way as to erase individuality, hair may be shaved or allowed to grow long. Neophytes are often isolated from the everyday world, and may undergo certain ordeals that bind them to one another and to those initiating them. Turner coined the term 'communitas' to describe a spontaneous, immediate, and concrete relatedness that is typical of people in the liminal stage of a rite of passage. Liminality can also be institutionalized and extended almost indefinitely, as for instance in the military, monastic communities, hospitals, or asylums.

MALE AND FEMALE INITIATION

Bruce Lincoln has criticized both van Gennep and Turner's models as more relevant to male than female initiations, pointing out that women have little status in the social hierarchy, and therefore the middle stage of a woman's initiation is less likely to stress anti-structural elements. Rather than being brought low as a prelude to being elevated, her lowlier place within society is reinforced. A woman is more likely than her male counterparts to be initiated singly, and to be enclosed within a domestic space. Women are generally adorned rather than stripped, and the nature of the knowledge

passed on during initiation is likely to be mundane rather than esoteric. Rather than separation, liminality, and reintegration, Lincoln proposes that for women initiation is more likely to involve enclosure, metamorphosis or magnification, and emergence.

Malagasy children, Madagascar.

A ritual is a type of performance, but not all performances are rituals. Richard Schechner (b. 1934) has pointed out that whether a performance is to be classified as ritual or theatre depends on the context. If the purpose of a performance is to be efficacious, it is a ritual. If its purpose is to entertain, it is theatre. These are not absolute distinctions, and most performances contain elements of both efficacious intention and entertainment. At the ritual end of the continuum we are likely to have an active 'audience', who share the aims and intentions of the main actors. Time and space are sacred, and symbolically marked, and it is the end result of the action that matters — to heal, initiate, aid the deceased, or whatever it may be. In a theatrical performance, the audience is more likely to observe than participate, and the event is an end in itself. It is performed for those watching, and not for, or in the presence of, a higher power or absent other.

FIONA BOWIE

QUESTIONS

1. What is a religion, and why can the term be problematic?

2. Why did many phenomenologists reject theological approaches to religion?

3. An atheist will always be a more objective student of religion than a believer. How far do you agree or disagree with this statement?

4. What problems might you encounter in studying a religion as an outsider?

5. What did Marx mean when he referred to religion as 'the sigh of the oppressed creature'?

6. How do Marx and Weber differ in their perceptions of religion?

7. Explain Durkheim's view of the role of religion in society.

8. Why has there been renewed interest in the sociology of religion in recent years?

9. What can psychology tell us about why people may hold religious beliefs?

10. How has Critical Theory influenced our understanding of religion since the 1960s?

FURTHER READING

Connolly, Peter (ed.), *Approaches to the Study of Religion*. London: Continuum, 2001.

Eliade, Mircea, *The Sacred and the Profane: The Nature of Religion*. New York: Harcourt, Brace, 1959.

Fitzgerald, Timothy, *The Ideology of Religious Studies*. Oxford: Oxford University Press, 2000.

Flood, Gavin, *Beyond Phenomenology: Rethinking the Study of Religion*. London: Cassell, 1999.

Geertz, Clifford, 'Religion as a Cultural System', in Michael Banton, ed., *Anthropological Approaches to the Study of Religion*, pp. 1–46. London: Tavistock, 1966.

Kunin, Seth D., *Religion: The Modern Theories*. Baltimore: Johns Hopkins University Press, 2003.

Levi-Strauss, Claude, *Myth and Meaning*. Toronto: University of Toronto Press, 1978.

McCutcheon, Russell T. ed., *The Insider/Outsider Problem in the Study of Religion*. London: Cassell, 1999.

Otto, Rudolf, *The Idea of the Holy*. London: Oxford University Press, 1923.

Pals, Daniel L., *Eight Theories of Religion*. New York: Oxford University Press, 2006.

Van der Leeuw, Gerardus, *Religion in Essence and Manifestation*. London: Allen & Unwin, 1938.

TIMELINE OF WORLD RELIGIONS

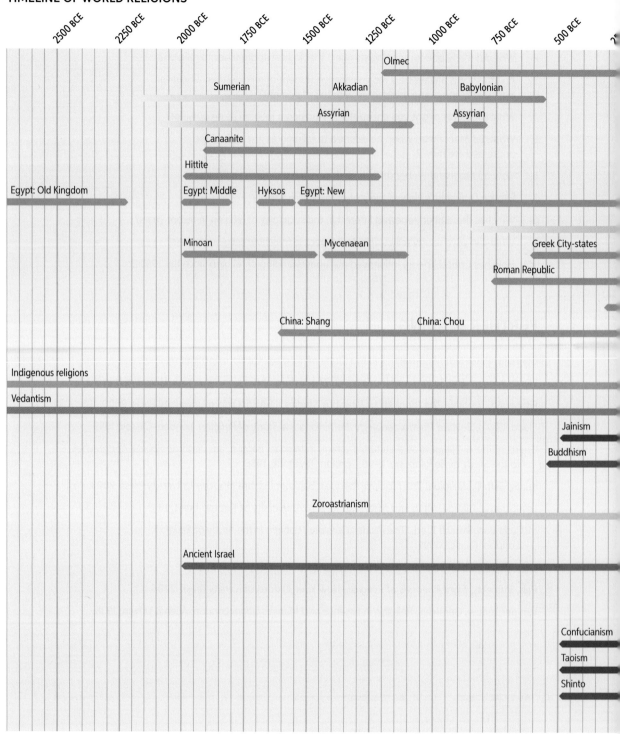

| 2500 BCE | 2250 BCE | 2000 BCE | 1750 BCE | 1500 BCE | 1250 BCE | 1000 BCE | 750 BCE | 500 BCE |

Olmec

Sumerian   Akkadian   Babylonian

Assyrian   Assyrian

Canaanite

Hittite

Egypt: Old Kingdom   Egypt: Middle   Hyksos   Egypt: New

Minoan   Mycenaean   Greek City-states

Roman Republic

China: Shang   China: Chou

Indigenous religions

Vedantism

Jainism

Buddhism

Zoroastrianism

Ancient Israel

Confucianism

Taoism

Shinto

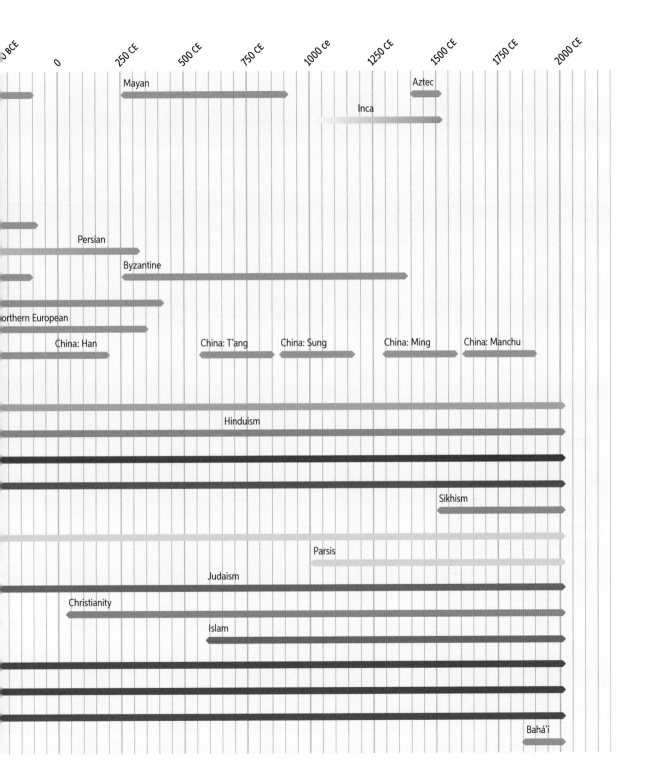

BCE	0	250 CE	500 CE	750 CE	1000 ce	1250 CE	1500 CE	1750 CE	2000 CE

Mayan

Aztec

Inca

Persian

Byzantine

Northern European

China: Han

China: T'ang

China: Sung

China: Ming

China: Manchu

Hinduism

Sikhism

Parsis

Judaism

Christianity

Islam

Bahá'í

TIMELINE OF WORLD RELIGIONS

47

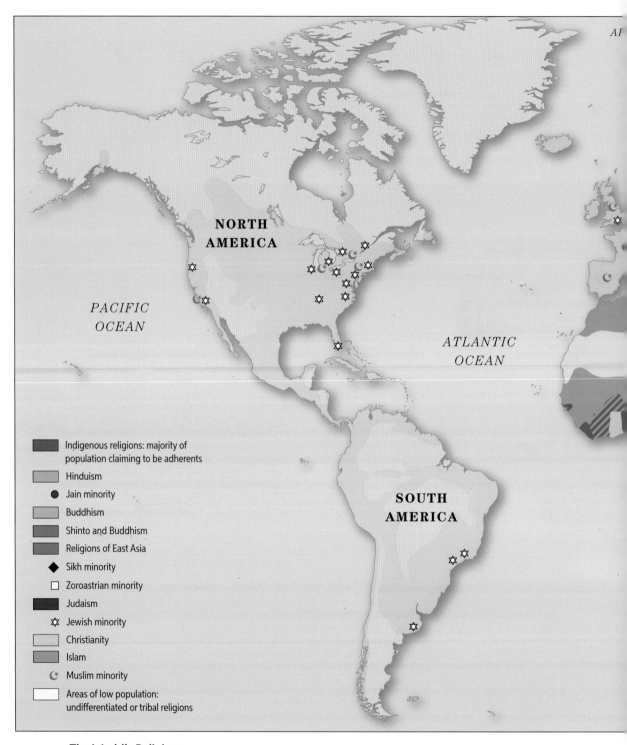

The World's Religions

Legend:

- Indigenous religions: majority of population claiming to be adherents
- Hinduism
- ● Jain minority
- Buddhism
- Shinto and Buddhism
- Religions of East Asia
- ◆ Sikh minority
- ☐ Zoroastrian minority
- Judaism
- ✡ Jewish minority
- Christianity
- Islam
- ☾ Muslim minority
- Areas of low population: undifferentiated or tribal religions

PACIFIC OCEAN

ATLANTIC OCEAN

NORTH AMERICA

SOUTH AMERICA

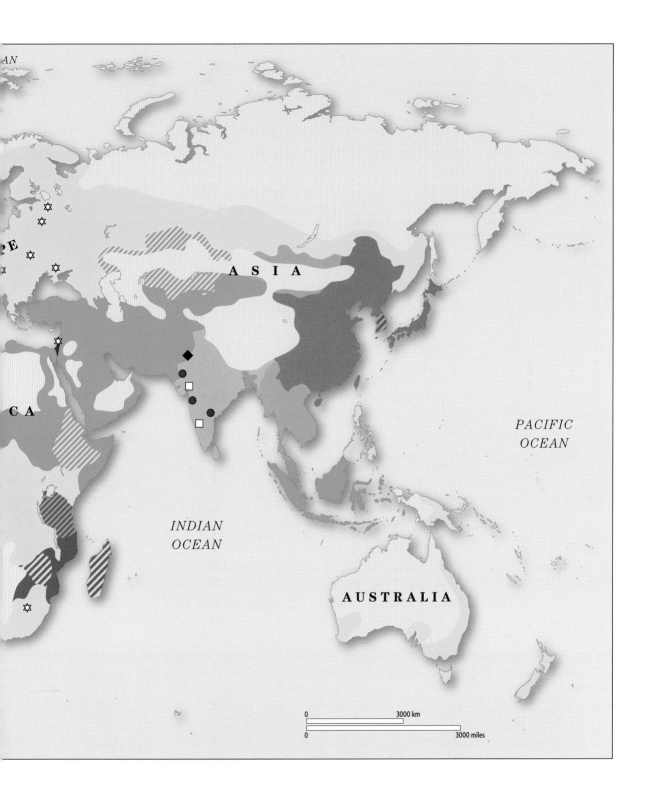

ASIA

PACIFIC
OCEAN

INDIAN
OCEAN

AUSTRALIA

0   3000 km

0   3000 miles

PART 2
HINDUISM

SUMMARY

The religion today known as Hinduism may be almost as old as Indian civilization itself: archaeological evidence suggests continuities between the religion of the Indus Valley society of 2500–1500 BCE and the Hinduism of today. The Vedic texts, from the period that followed, provide the basis for some of the central themes of Hindu belief, including *samsara*, the doctrine that all creatures are reborn repeatedly unless the cycle can be broken through liberation (*moksha*), and *karma*, the notion that actions in one life are rewarded or punished in the next. The Vedic religion was hierarchical, and centred around sacrificial offerings. In time, sacrifice was largely replaced by *puja*, the personal devotion of an individual to a particular deity.

Hinduism has a vast body of sacred texts, from the early Vedas onward, and generally is divided into the more authoritative *Sruti* – revealed scripture – and the less authoritative *Smriti* – which includes Epics such as the *Mahabharata* (including the *Bhagavad Gita*) and the *Ramayana*. A hierarchy of sorts also exists amongst the many gods of India, with Vishnu and Shiva enjoying a privileged position – although there is no consensus as to whether there are in fact many gods, or whether the many are merely different representations of the one God, *Brahman*.

Today, like so many religions, Hinduism has a following throughout the world, largely because of the many Indian diaspora communities. Despite this, the subcontinent remains hugely important for Hindus, in part because of the value placed on the many sacred sites in the country, such as the River Ganges, and in part because of the strong ties that bind the wider community. Within India itself – now a secular democracy – there exists something of a division between those at ease with recent developments, such as secularization and the changing role of women, and the emergent Hindu nationalists – often deeply hostile to other religions in the region, particularly Islam – who seek a stronger role for religion in public life.

CHAPTER 9

A Historical Overview

The term 'Hinduism' as we understand it today refers to the majority religion of the Indian subcontinent. The present understanding of Hinduism as a 'world religion' has come about only since the nineteenth century, when Hindu reformers and Western orientalists came to refer to the diverse beliefs and practices characterizing religious life in South Asia as 'Hinduism'. Yet this classification is problematic, as Hinduism possesses many features characteristic of 'indigenous religions': it has no single historical founder, no central revelation, no creed or unified system of belief, no single doctrine of salvation, and no centralized authority. In this sense, it is different from other 'world religions'. Huge diversity and variety of religious movements, systems, beliefs, and practices are all characteristic features of 'Hinduism'. Also, there is no clear division between the 'sacred' and 'profane' — or natural and supernatural: religion and social life are inseparable and intertwined. Nevertheless, most scholars would agree there are unifying strands that run through the diverse traditions that constitute it. Although the term Hinduism is recent, the diverse traditions that it encompasses have very ancient origins that extend back beyond the second millennium BCE.

> *Hinduism is a living organism liable to growth and decay and subject to the laws of nature. One and indivisible at the root, it has grown into a vast tree with innumerable branches.*
>
> Mahatma Gandhi, *Hindu Dharma* (New Delhi: Orient Paperbacks, 1987).

THE INDUS VALLEY CIVILIZATION

The earliest traces of Hinduism can be found in the Indus Valley civilization which flourished from 2500 to about 1500 BCE along the banks of the River Indus, which flows through present-day Pakistan. Archaeological excavations in this area have revealed evidence of what appears to be a highly developed urban culture with sophisticated water distribution, drainage and garbage disposal technologies and well-developed systems of farming, grain-storage and pottery. Little is known about the religion of this civilization. The large number of terracotta figurines unearthed through excavations suggest a continuity between the iconographic features of these images and those of such later Hindu deities as Shiva and the mother goddess. Given the lack of systematic evidence for such continuity, however,

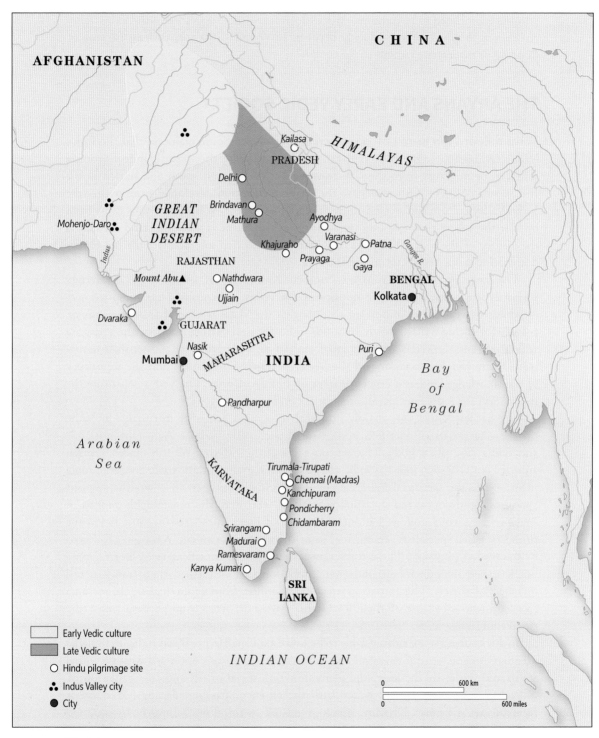

CHINA

AFGHANISTAN

HIMALAYAS

Kailasa

PRADESH

Delhi

Brindavan
Mathura

*GREAT
INDIAN
DESERT*

Mohenjo-Daro

Indus

Ayodhya

Khajuraho
Prayaga

Varanasi
Patna

Gaya

Ganges R.

BENGAL

Kolkata

RAJASTHAN

Mount Abu▲
Nathdwara
Ujjain

Dvaraka
GUJARAT

Nasik

Mumbai

MAHARASHTRA

INDIA

Puri

*Bay
of
Bengal*

Pandharpur

*Arabian
Sea*

KARNATAKA

Tirumala-Tirupati
Chennai (Madras)
Kanchipuram
Pondicherry
Chidambaram

Srirangam
Madurai
Ramesvaram
Kanya Kumari

**SRI
LANKA**

Early Vedic culture
Late Vedic culture
O Hindu pilgrimage site
•• Indus Valley city
● City

INDIAN OCEAN

0 —— 600 km
0 —— 600 miles

Hinduism

scholars are inclined to be cautious. Archaeological evidence suggests that the Indus Valley civilization declined rather suddenly between 1800 and 1700 BCE, perhaps because of flooding or inadequate rainfall.

THE ARYANS AND EARLY VEDIC SOCIETY

What followed is a matter of considerable controversy. Some maintain that the Indus Valley civilization came to be replaced by the culture of the Aryans, Indo-European invaders, or migrants from the Caucasus region, who moved south and settled in the Indian subcontinent. Others believe the Aryan civilization developed from within the Indus Valley culture and was not introduced from outside. Whether Aryans came from outside the subcontinent or not, the history of Hinduism as we understand it today is the history of the next 2000 years of Aryan culture, often interacting with, but always dominating, non-Aryan cultures in the area.

The language of the Aryans was Sanskrit. Knowledge of the early Aryans derives primarily from early Sanskrit compositions, the Vedas, a corpus of texts compiled over hundreds of years. It is important to note that the Vedas were oral for thousands of years before being written down. In South India, the oral performances of the Vedas are still important; the Vedas are articulated, embodied, and performed, rather than simply read. Many Hindus today regard the Vedas as timeless revelation and the repository of all knowledge, and as a crucial marker of Hindu identity. The Vedas constitute the foundation for most later developments in Hinduism.

The earliest Vedas were mainly liturgical texts, used primarily in ritual. The Vedic rituals were rituals of sacrifice, addressed to such early gods as Agni (the fire god) and Soma (the plant god). The central act was the offering of substances – often animals, but also such items as milk, clarified butter, grain, and the hallucinogenic soma plant – into the sacrificial fire. The ritual was usually initiated by a wealthy sponsor (*yajamana*), and conducted by ritual specialists, who were the most highly ranked in Vedic society, which followed a fourfold system of hierarchical classification. Below the priests or ritual specialists (Brahmans) came the warriors or rulers (*Kshatriyas*), followed by the traders (*Vaishyas*). These three classes (*varna*) were known as 'twice-born' (*dvija*), because their male members underwent initiation that confirmed their status as full members of society. This initiation rite separated them from a fourth class, the servants (*Shudras*), who – because of their 'low' status – were debarred from perpetuating Vedic ritual traditions.

In due course, Aryan culture came to be well established in northern India. Brahmanic ideology became central to social and political life, and was concerned with the ritual status and duties of the king, the maintaining of social order, and the regulation of individual behaviour in accordance with the all-encompassing ideology of duty, or righteousness (*dharma*). Dharmic ideology related to ritual and moral behaviour, and defined good conduct according to such factors as one's class (*varna*) and one's stage of life (*ashrama*). It operated simultaneously at several levels: the transcendental, and therefore eternal (*sanatana dharma*), the everyday (*sadharana dharma*), and the individual and personal (*svadharma*). Neglecting *dharma* was believed to lead to undesirable social, as well as personal, consequences.

THE LATER VEDIC PERIOD

Alongside the performance of Vedic ritual, speculation arose about its meaning and purpose. These speculations were developed in the later Vedic texts – the *Aranyakas* and *Upanishads* – which tended to see the observance of ritual action as secondary to the gaining of spiritual knowledge. Central to this approach was the *karma-samsara-moksha* doctrine:
• all beings are reincarnated into the world (*samsara*) over and over again;
• the results of action (*karma*) are reaped in future lives;
• this process of endless rebirth is characterized by suffering (*dukkha*);
• liberation (*moksha*) from this suffering can be obtained by gaining spiritual knowledge.

Gaining spiritual knowledge thus came to assume central importance, and the self-disciplining and methods of asceticism necessary for gaining it were developed in Hinduism's traditions of yoga and world renunciation. Ascetic groups known as strivers (*sramanas*) were formed during this period, seeking liberation through austerity. Buddhism and Jainism, both of which rejected the authority of the Vedas, originated in these groups. Whereas monastic institutions developed in Buddhism from its inception, similar institutions appeared within the Hindu pale only later, possibly in the eighth and ninth centuries CE, when – according to Hindu belief – the theologian Shankara (c. 788–820 CE) founded monastic centres in the four corners of India, and instituted the first renunciatory order of the Dasanamis.

Alongside early Hinduism's elaboration of systems of ritual, and its teachings about liberation/salvation involving yoga and meditation, there developed highly sophisticated philosophical systems, the *darshanas*, comprising mainly Samkhya and Yoga, Mimamsa and Vedanta, and Nyaya and Vaisheshika. These in turn generated a multitude of metaphysical positions, and traditions of rigorous philosophical debate, within the parameters of Vedic revelation and the doctrine of liberation. One of the most important of these Indian philosophical traditions today is the philosophy of non-dualism (*advaita vedanta*), propounded by Shankara, the most famous of Indian philosopher-theologians.

SECTARIAN WORSHIP

Through much of the first millennium CE, sectarian worship of particular deities grew and flourished in India. Vedic sacrifice came to be increasingly marginalized, giving way – though never disappearing completely – to devotional worship or *puja*. *Puja* is a ritual expression of love or devotion (*bhakti*) to a deity, often a personal god or goddess, with whom the devotee establishes an intense and intimate relationship. Corresponding to the growth of Hindu theism and devotionalism, Sanskrit narrative traditions grew and flourished, the most important of which were the Hindu epics or *itihasas* – the *Ramayana* and the *Mahabharata* – the Puranas – devotional texts containing, among other things, mythological stories about the gods and goddesses, and treatises on ritual worship – and devotional poetry in several Indian regional languages, most notably Tamil. One of the most important developments at this time was the composition of the *Bhagavad Gita*, the 'Song of the Lord', contained in the *Mahabharata*. This work, perhaps the most famous of the Hindu scriptures, expresses in narrative form the concerns of Hinduism: the importance of *dharma*, responsible action, and the maintenance of social order and stability, combined with the importance of devotion to the transcendent as a personal god.

Temple cities grew and flourished in this period, serving not only as commercial and administrative hubs of kingdoms, but as ritual centres, with the temple located at the heart of the town and, therefore, of the kingdom. Kings sought to derive legitimacy for their rule through their royal patronage of these ritual sites, dedicated to one or the other of the major Puranic deities. Large temple complexes stood testimony to a king's dharmic rule over his kingdom, which was often modelled on the ideal of divine kingship symbolized by the great god Vishnu. Sectarian devotional groups emerged, dedicated to the worship of Vishnu (*Vaishnavas*), Shiva (*Shaivas*), and the goddess Devi (*Shaktas*).

HINDUISM DURING BRITISH COLONIAL RULE

These theistic traditions continued to flourish, to lesser or greater degrees, through much of the following period, when large sections of the Indian subcontinent were conquered and ruled by Muslim rulers. The rule of the last Muslim emperor in India came to an end in the eighteenth century, and British forces, initially in the form of the East India Company, and later the British crown, stepped in to assume power. By the middle of the eighteenth century, British power was at its peak. Hindu traditions, which had tended to be relatively insular in the intervening period, now responded actively to the British and, more importantly, Christian presence in their midst. Hindu reform movements arose, led by such figures as Ram Mohan Roy (1772–1883), Dayananda Sarasvati (1824–83), and Vivekananda (1863–1902), all seeking to restore the perceived glory of Hinduism's ancient past. It was at this time that Hinduism came to be defined in the terms by which we understand it today – a world religion, with a distinct identity. These reform movements, often collectively referred to as the Hindu renaissance, absorbed Christianity's rationalist elements, and paid particular attention to social and ethical concerns. Most of these movements were closely linked with the increasingly vocal Indian nationalist movement, which brought about the end of British colonial rule, and established India as an independent nation state in 1947.

RELIGIOUS NATIONALISM IN CONTEMPORARY INDIA

Though India defined itself as a secular state on gaining independence, it has experienced a resurgence of religious nationalism, particularly since the 1980s, expressed in *Hindutva* ('Hinduness'), the ideology of Hindu nationalists who call for a state in which civic rights, nationhood, and national culture would be defined by Hinduism. Their politicized, activist religious nationalism has precedents in various movements of organized Hinduism that arose in British India. Today the Sangh Parivar, a 'family' of social and political organizations, works to propagate *Hindutva*, with its political wing, the Bharatiya Janata Party (BJP, 'Indian People's Party'), winning enough support to head a coalition government between 1998 and 2004.

A significant act of religious violence in recent times was the destruction of the Mughal Babri mosque in Ayodhya in 1992, by supporters of *Hindutva* demanding the setting up of a temple dedicated to the Hindu deity Rama at the site, which they believe to be Rama's birthplace. Several violent incidents between Hindus and Muslims have been precipitated by this temple/mosque controversy.

BEYOND INDIA'S FRONTIERS

Yet many Hindus are not greatly concerned, as 'Hindu-ness' is not something they explicitly think about. Running counter to these chauvinist and violently exclusivist forms of Hinduism, other forms of Hindu belief and practice adopt a more inclusive, universal orientation, emphasizing values such as social justice, peace, and the spiritual transformation of humanity – though Hinduism has in fact always been inclusive, encompassing many traditions and practices. Some recent manifestations of Hinduism, especially in the form of Indian gurus addressing Western and/or multicultural audiences, have transcended nationalistic boundaries in their teaching and philosophy.

Hinduism has also transcended national boundaries in another sense. While Hinduism has long flourished beyond the Indian subcontinent, in places such as Java and Bali, in the twentieth century the Hindu diaspora spread markedly, establishing communities in host cultures across the globe. This geographical transcendence of boundaries does not always parallel ideological dispositions and orientations, however. Religious nationalism often strikes deep roots in diaspora communities, such that India as a geographical entity comes to be perceived, in the imagination of Hindus abroad, as their sacred, or holy, land, which they identify with conceptions of a Hindu religious polity, and therefore a Hindu nation state.

MAYA WARRIER

HINDUISM TIMELINE

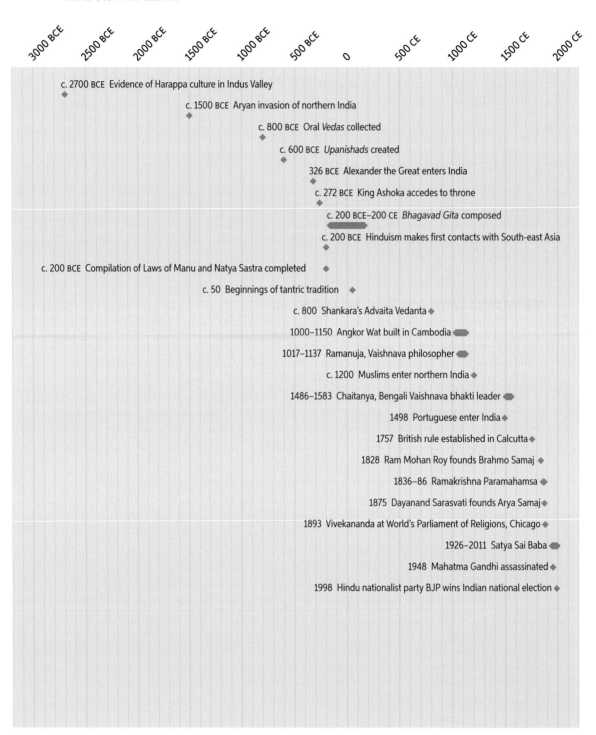

3000 BCE	2500 BCE	2000 BCE	1500 BCE	1000 BCE	500 BCE	0	500 CE	1000 CE	1500 CE	2000 CE

c. 2700 BCE Evidence of Harappa culture in Indus Valley

c. 1500 BCE Aryan invasion of northern India

c. 800 BCE Oral *Vedas* collected

c. 600 BCE *Upanishads* created

326 BCE Alexander the Great enters India

c. 272 BCE King Ashoka accedes to throne

c. 200 BCE–200 CE *Bhagavad Gita* composed

c. 200 BCE Hinduism makes first contacts with South-east Asia

c. 200 BCE Compilation of Laws of Manu and Natya Sastra completed

c. 50 Beginnings of tantric tradition

c. 800 Shankara's Advaita Vedanta

1000–1150 Angkor Wat built in Cambodia

1017–1137 Ramanuja, Vaishnava philosopher

c. 1200 Muslims enter northern India

1486–1583 Chaitanya, Bengali Vaishnava bhakti leader

1498 Portuguese enter India

1757 British rule established in Calcutta

1828 Ram Mohan Roy founds Brahmo Samaj

1836–86 Ramakrishna Paramahamsa

1875 Dayanand Sarasvati founds Arya Samaj

1893 Vivekananda at World's Parliament of Religions, Chicago

1926–2011 Satya Sai Baba

1948 Mahatma Gandhi assassinated

1998 Hindu nationalist party BJP wins Indian national election

CHAPTER 10

Philosophy

Hindu philosophy, the oldest continuing tradition of Indian thought, stretches back to sacred texts written between 900 and 400 BCE known as the *Upanishads* — literally 'to sit beneath', as at the feet of a teacher. These texts are reflections on the deeper meaning of the rites, hymns, and ritual prescriptions found in earlier Vedic writings. However, they were soon regarded as a genre of Vedic literature in their own right, and it is here that we first encounter a developed theory of *karma* (action, making; law of cause and effect) and *moksha* (liberation from the cycle of rebirth).

THE *ASTIKA* SCHOOLS

Hindu philosophy developed through debate between schools of Hindu thought and, importantly, with Jain, Carvaka (materialist), and Buddhist thinkers. During the classical period of Hindu philosophy (100 BCE to 1000 CE) the six *astika* schools ('orthodox', in accepting Vedic authority) condensed and cemented their distinctive views. These are usually paired:

- *Purva-mimamsa* — Vedanta
- *Samkhya* — Yoga
- *Nyaya* — *Vaisheshika*

> *The wise call him a man of learning whose every activity is free from desire and specific intention; his actions are consumed in the fire of knowledge.*
>
> *Bhagavad Gita 4:19*

It should be noted that these pairings bring together a larger number of schools, and are less to do with Indian philosophical schools themselves, and more the result of the way Indian thought has been studied in the West since the nineteenth century.

While it greatly oversimplifies historical Indian thought to impute consensus, it is useful to isolate a few central notions that serve as building blocks for the six 'orthodox' philosophical perspectives (*darshanas*) above. A key philosophical question in Indian thought, addressing, among other issues, being (ontology), knowledge (epistemology), morality (ethics), God (theology), and even beauty (aesthetics), is 'Who are we?' To understand the various responses, we need to consider three central presuppositions of Hindu thought:

- the cyclical nature of time
- an essential connection between microcosmic and macrocosmic levels of reality
- a principle of causality

In Hindu philosophy the universe has neither beginning nor end. It issued forth from *Brahman* (the ultimate, divine 'ground of Being'), and will eventually return to *Brahman*, only to repeat the cycle again. If time itself revolves in an endless cycle, then all of creation also exists in a cyclical way. So life is followed by death, giving rise to a new life, and so on. This cycle of birth and rebirth (*samsara*) is deducible from any observation of the natural world, and is an example of how events at the microcosmic level of individual lives, seasons, and generations are seen to be intimately connected to the macrocosmic level of the great ages of history (*yugas*), the cosmic creations and dissolutions, and indeed time itself. Furthermore, the causal principle of *karma* connects each event in *samsara*, so that events in this cycle affect events in subsequent cycles, just as they themselves are already affected by events in previous cycles. Time, causality, and the micro- macrocosm are linked: what one does, and how one chooses, has a necessary – if miniscule – effect on the entire universe.

DHARMA AND *MOKSHA*

The three presuppositions inform two other primary concepts: *dharma* and *moksha*.
- *Dharma* ('to uphold') is understood to be the moral and metaphysical foundation of the universe. Acting in accordance with one's *dharma*, which is not always easy to determine, connects one's activities and life to one's social structure and environment. Fulfilling one's dharmic duties is necessary, but not sufficient, for *moksha*.
- To attain *moksha* – ultimate liberation, the goal of human existence – is to attain complete freedom from the samsaric cycle of birth and rebirth, and all the dissatisfaction, suffering, and death – as well as the joys and pleasures – which go with it.

The *Samkhya*–Yoga school sees *moksha* as one's return, through yogic discipline, to an original, blissful state of pure spirit (*purusha*), separated from matter (*prakriti*). For the *Nyaya*–*Vaisheshika* school, more interested in logical reasoning and the right understanding of reality, *moksha* is gained through right understanding of the universe, and of one's real nature as a simple collection of material and non-material qualities: it means returning to an undifferentiated state of being; free from change and suffering – a vision harshly criticized by the *Mimamsa*–Vedanta school, which compared it to the existence of a stone. This last school saw *moksha* as the fulfilment of one's dharmic duty, resulting in the cessation of rebirth, and the realization of one's true relationship with *Brahman*.

VEDANTA

Only Vedanta now commands a large following. Of the dozen or so Vedantic schools, three are of particular interest:
- *Advaita* (non-dualism)
- *Vishishtadvaita* (non-dualism of particulars)
- *Dvaita* (dualism)

The great Hindu philosopher-saint Shankara (c. 788–820 CE) expounded an austerely non-dualistic (*advaita*) system. In his short life, he established monasteries in the four corners of India, and a monastic order of ten divisions, and was held by some of his followers to be an incarnation of the Hindu deity Shiva. He has had inordinate influence on modern Hinduism, through such Neo-Vedantic exponents as Dayananda Sarasvati (1824–83), Swami Vivekananda (1863–1902), and even Gandhi (1869–1948). *Advaita* holds that one's true self (*atman*) is literally identical to *Brahman*. Whereas Judaism, Christianity, and Islam are dualistic, maintaining a strong distinction between God and the human soul, between God and the world, and between the individual and the world, for Shankara's *advaita Vedanta*, all is one, and any perceived dualism is the result of ignorance. We are working within an illusory interpretation (*maya*) of the world, but through the hearing and study of the Vedas – particularly the *Upanishads*, the *Bhagavad Gita*, and the *Brahmasutras* – we can come to a correct and liberating knowledge of the world and of our own true nature as identical with *Brahman*.

Ramanuja (1077–1157) is often compared with Thomas Aquinas (1225–74), such was the depth and subtlety of their respective systems. Ramanuja revered the South Indian poet/saint traditions of the Alvars, and proposed that, although

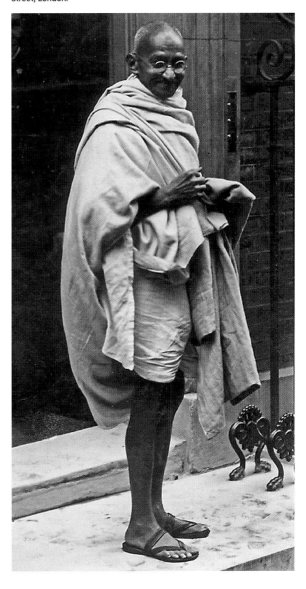

Mahatma Gandhi, Indian nationalist leader and proponent of non-violent civil disobedience, outside 10 Downing Street, London.

identical to *Brahman*, the individual *atman* retains its particular qualities, just as a unified body retains its particular parts (*Vishishtadvaita*). He recognized that simultaneous unity and difference (*bheda-abheda*) is essential in a monotheistic tradition which claims ultimate unity between God and the devotee, but also values devotional love towards God.

Madhva (c. 1197–1276) wrote commentaries on a number of sacred texts, and established a new, dualistic interpretation of Vedanta. The *dvaita vedanta* school maintains that the perfect *Brahman* could not be identical to the imperfect, created *atman*: there must be a fundamental distinction between the individual self and God. One can only talk of such identity in the way one talks of the relationship between a devoted lover and his or her beloved. A Vaishnavite, Madhva took both the evidence of our senses and the reality of difference seriously. Any view which claimed real unity with the divine threatened the transcendence of God, and undervalued our own experience.

There was – and remains – lively debate. The question of who we ultimately are provided for Hindu philosophers a gateway into profound discussions of the nature of reality, knowledge, truth, and goodness which continue to guide and instruct today.

TINU RUPARELL

CHAPTER 11

Sacred Writings

Hindu scriptures comprise a vast corpus of literature, dating from 1300 BCE to modern times. Most of the scriptures are in Sanskrit — a word meaning 'refined' — a classical Indian language now used only by scholars and for ritual purposes. There is also a considerable amount of religious literature in regional Indian languages, and variants of the original texts, which emphasize a particular aspect of Hindu belief. For example, the *Adhyatma Ramayana* is a version of the popular epic *Ramayana* that stresses devotion (*bhakti*). What follows does not exhaust the many diverse categories of Hindu sacred writings, but outlines the major elements of a vast array of texts, dealing with various aspects of belief, ritual, and tradition in Hindu society.

Hindus generally divide their scriptures into two categories: heard or revealed (*Sruti*) and remembered (*Smriti*). *Sruti* scriptures are believed to be communicated directly by God to ancient Indian sages; *Smriti* scriptures are less authoritative, and consist of texts such as the Hindu epics —the *Ramayana*, and the *Mahabharata*; the *Dharma Sutras* — books of law, concerned with customs and correct conduct — and *Puranas* — mythology.

THE VEDAS

The Hindu canon is usually termed Veda, from the root *vid*, meaning 'knowledge'. The Vedas comprise four main types: The Vedic *Samhitas*, *Brahmanas*, *Aranyakas*, and *Upanishads*.

1. The Vedic *Samhitas*, classified as the *Rig*, *Sama*, *Yajur* and *Atharva* Vedas, are the earliest known Hindu religious literature (1300–200 BCE), consisting mainly of praises to various deities of ancient Hinduism, led by Indra, king of the gods.
2. The *Brahmanas* stipulate the details of, and explain the significance of, rituals (*yaga* or *yajna*), especially the fire ritual, in which oblations were poured out, or cast into fire, to be conveyed to the gods. The prominence of Agni, the god of fire, and of the Brahman priest in these texts indicates the growing importance and complexity of the fire ritual in early Indian religion.
3. The *Aranyakas* ('forest books') provide analysis and interpretation of the fire ritual, whereby a correspondence is drawn between the ritual and the cosmos. The ritual, moreover, is understood to have an intrinsic power, by which the gods are to some extent bypassed. Indeed, the *Aranyakas* also represent a transition from the

ritualistic *Brahmanas* to the far more contemplative and philosophical themes of the *Upanishads*, tending to move away from the polytheism of the *Samhitas* towards a more philosophical, monistic, or pantheistic understanding of reality, in which despite appearances all is one. Hence, the *Aranyakas* and the *Upanishads* mark a growing resistance to the ritualism of the fire sacrifice, and a preference for more contemplative and spiritual forms of worship.

4. The *Upanishads* (*upa* = alongside, *nishad* = set) are commentaries and elaborations of the ideas encountered in the Vedic *Samhitas* and *Brahmanas*. Four major themes can be identified: internal sacrifice, the idea of the *atman* (similar to 'soul' or 'self'), *Brahman* (non-personal divine being), and monistic theology, which equates the *atman*, and indeed the whole cosmos, with *Brahman* — everything is *Brahman*. The previous emphasis on the importance and intricacy of the fire ritual is overshadowed by an emphasis on personal spiritual development. In religious terminology, *tapas* or *pranagnihotra* — sometimes described as the oblation of one's body in the fire of one's breath — is shown as much more efficacious and powerful than the external *yajna*. The *atman-Brahman* identification has tremendous implications for the Hindu's understanding of the nature of God, the cosmos, and the liberation — or 'salvation' — of the individual.

> Then was not non-existence nor existence: there was no realm of air, no sky beyond it. What stirred, and where? What gave shelter? Was water there, unfathomed depth of water?
>
> Death was not then, nor was there anything immortal: no sign was there of the day's and night's divider. That One, breathless, breathed by its own nature: apart from it was nothing whatsoever.
>
> Darkness there was: at first concealed in darkness this. All was indiscriminate chaos. All that existed then was void and formless: by the great power of heat was born that One.
>
> Thereafter rose Desire in the beginning, Desire, the primal seed and germ of Spirit. Sages who searched with their heart's thought discovered the bond of existence in the non-existent . . .
>
> Who truly knows and who can here declare it, whence it was born and whence comes this creation? The gods came later than this world's creation. Who knows then whence it first came into being?
>
> He, the first origin of this creation, whether he formed it all or did not form it, Whose eye controls this world in highest heaven, he verily knows it, or perhaps he knows not.
>
> The Creation Hymn, *Rig Veda* 10.129, transl. Ralph T. H. Griffith, 1896, adapted

DHARMA SUTRAS

Of the *Dharma Sutras* (literally, aphorisms relating to duties), the most important is the compendium of law known as *Manava Dharma Shastra* (The laws of Manu), which stipulate the duties, laws, and regulations binding on all categories of Hindus, whatever their caste (*varna*), stage of life (*ashrama*), or gender. Because ideas of salvation in Hinduism involve adherence to these laws, regulations, and duties, it is vital for Hindus to know and understand them. In other words, devout Hindus seeking release from *samsara* – the cycle of lives, deaths, and reincarnations – need to obey the *Dharma Sutras*.

THE EPICS

Perusal of the two epics of Hinduism, the *Ramayana* and the *Mahabharata*, is deemed a sacred duty, and helpful in progressing towards liberation/salvation (*moksha*) from the cycle of worldly life. These epics, allegedly written by the ancient sages Valmiki and Vyasa, are deemed by scholars to be compilations of folk-tales, songs sung by minstrels, and heroic stories composed in honour of kings. However, the editing of these scriptures was highly skilful and, despite their complexity and bewildering multiplicity of themes, they seem to point to a central theme of salvation of the world, and the continual war between good and evil in the universe. The stories are threaded into a central theme of a world slowly, but inexorably, declining to an age of destruction. The Battle of Kurukshetra is a climactic event in the *Mahabharata*, for instance, marking the beginning of the age of evil (*Kaliyuga*), and witnessing the gradual decline of honour, compassion, and chivalry during its denouement. In the *Ramayana*, the war between Rama and Ravana symbolizes the confrontation between the forces of good and evil in the world. In both, the principal characters are either gods or demi-gods and demons. Although the gods ultimately win, they have to compromise, and often resort to devious stratagems to achieve their victory. The end result is a tainted world, in which even the gods are not entirely free from unethical actions.

Both epics have common features: a righteous prince excluded from kingship and exiled; a climactic battle between forces of good and evil; the intervention of God on behalf of the good; in spite of many reverses, the ultimate triumph of good over evil. The epics present many ideals and heroic role models to Hindus, and are generally Vaishnavite, extolling the god Vishnu.

THE *BHAGAVAD GITA*

The *Bhagavad Gita* ('song of the Lord') is a small part of the epic *Mahabharata*. Nevertheless, it is a highly influential scripture within Hinduism, and has acquired almost an independent standing of its own. It is a discourse between Krishna, the incarnation (*avatar*) of the god Vishnu, and his devotee Prince Arjuna, the greatest warrior in the *Mahabharata*. The discussion is obviously an insertion into the epic, and many scholars consider it to be an *Upanishad*.

Above all, the *Bhagavad Gita* is an irenic scripture, which seeks to unite the major theological strands of Hinduism. It says that all ways to salvation are equally valid: the way of enlightenment (*jnana marga*), the way of altruistic righteous action and progression through the caste hierarchy (*nishkama karma marga*), the way of meditation (*yoga marga*), and the way of devotion (*bhakti marga*). However, it argues that the way of devotion (*bhakti*) is the highest of all paths and – for the first time in Hinduism – it reveals that the devotee is greatly loved by a gracious God. Consequently, it also proposes a radical rethinking of traditional Hindu concepts of salvation (*moksha*), in that it argues that it is open to all castes, and to men and women.

THE *PURANAS*

The *Puranas* – 'ancient stories' – are, again, a vast body of literature. Traditionally, there are eighteen *Puranas* which have been classified as associated with the gods Vishnu, Brahma, and Shiva, as well as many associated with minor deities and with holy places, such as particular temples or sacred sites. The contents are wide-ranging, including, for example, genealogies, law codes, descriptions of rituals, and pilgrimages to holy places. They are not merely a collection of old tales, as the name *Purana* seems to suggest, but narratives that highlight a theistic stance and vision.

THEODORE GABRIEL

CHAPTER 12

Beliefs

What we now know as Hinduism has developed into a rich, pluralist religious culture, with a great variety of customs, forms of worship, gods and goddesses, theologies, philosophies, stories, art, and music. Many Hindus believe its essential teachings remain the same down the centuries; however, diversity within Hinduism has led some scholars to talk of Hindu religions rather than a single Hindu religion, 'Hinduisms' rather than 'Hinduism', and even to abandon the term 'Hinduism' altogether. Moreover, many different Hindu voices and traditions compete globally to define the essential beliefs of Hinduism.

Hindus generally accept that they share common beliefs, principles, and structures. For many, however, Hinduism is not so much a system of beliefs as a way of life, a religious culture, a spiritual and intellectual quest, and an intense identification with the myriad ways in which the sacred is present in India. If asked about their beliefs, they often begin by talking about ethical teachings: kindness and truth; hospitality to the guest; respect for the family – and particularly for elders and parents. They may go on to consider beliefs in particular gods or goddesses, the authority of important sacred texts, the merit of pilgrimage, or the doctrine of *karma*. Some – not all – may accept the social hierarchy of the four *varnas* (caste system) and certain principles of purity and pollution. Any study of popular Hindu beliefs begins with the gods and goddesses of Hinduism.

GOD, GODS, AND GODDESSES

Hindus may be polytheistic, monotheistic, or monistic – believing that all reality is actually one. There are even orthodox Hindus who are atheistic. Many Hindus believe there is one God (*Brahman*) who can be worshipped in many forms. God can, for example, appear as a baby, a friend, a king, a mother, or a lover. God can manifest as male or female, or in non-human form; be worshipped as without form (*nirguna Brahman*) or with form (*saguna Brahman*); appear through icons and images (*murti*), or in human shape as a living saint or *guru*. Some Hindu gurus, such as Vivekananda (1863–1902), have even taught that God is embodied in the form of the universe, and in all sentient beings: hence, in serving others we are – quite literally – serving God.

Statue of Ganesha, the elephant-headed god.

God is sometimes understood in a threefold way, as *Trimurti*. The *Trimurti* consists of Brahma (the creator), Vishnu (the sustainer), and Shiva (the destroyer). However, not only is Brahma seldom worshipped, but nowadays the *Trimurti* is often replaced by a group of five gods: Vishnu, Shiva, Devi, Surya, and Ganesha.

The two pre-eminent gods, worshipped by Hindus everywhere, are Shiva and Vishnu. Vishnu is principally associated with the preservation of the cosmos and its proper order. He is, therefore, linked to kingship, and to the maintenance of *dharma* — law, order, righteousness. He is probably most frequently worshipped in his incarnations (*avatar*) as Rama and Krishna.

Shiva, 'the auspicious', is both the lord of *yogis* (ascetics) — depicted with matted hair, a body smeared with ashes, and meditating in a cremation ground — and also the divine lover. He is worshipped most commonly in the form of the phallus (*linga*). He has two sons: Ganesha, the elephant-headed god, and Skanda, or Murugan. Shiva reveals the ultimate nature of reality, the polarities of life and death, creation and destruction, the ascetic and the erotic, on whose interrelationship the whole of life depends.

Vaishnavism (devotion to Vishnu), Shaivism (devotion to Shiva), and Shaktism (devotion to the Goddess, or Devi) are the best-known traditions within Hinduism. However, Hindus often have a chosen deity (*ishtadev*) who, for the devotee, can take on the aspects of the ultimate god. Such gods and goddesses are worshipped both as distinct beings with their own stories and iconography, and as forms of the one ultimate reality (*Brahman*). Hindus may worship many gods, but they also believe all gods are one.

GODDESS WORSHIP

Goddess worship is one of the most distinctive traditions of Hinduism, going back to prehistoric times. *Shakti* (power, strength, force) is a term used to refer to the power of any deity, and is also the activating energy incarnated in goddesses. All goddesses can be seen as distinct deities, or as diverse forms of (Maha)devi, the (Great) Goddess. The Goddess (*Adyashakti*) is worshipped as the Supreme Being, but also as the consort of a male god.

A BRIEF INTRODUCTION TO HINDUISM

Detail of a statue of Shiva, displaying the dynamic feminine aspect of the supreme Divine, Shakti.

The consorts of the three great gods are Lakshmi, Sarasvati, and Parvati.

Sometimes scholars draw a distinction between independent goddesses, who are dangerous and 'hot', and wifely goddesses, who are restrained and 'cool'. For many Hindu women Sita, the wife of Rama, is the model Hindu wife, whose resolute integrity and courage are today emphasized by the Indian women's movement.

The land of India itself is worshipped as 'Divine Mother' (*Bharat Mata*), and is further sanctified by *Shaktipithas* (centres of Goddess worship), and by great rivers like the Ganges, which are worshipped as bestowers of prosperity and liberation.

AVATARS

Avatars are manifestations (literally 'descents') of God. They periodically intervene to fight evil, and ensure that the universe functions in accordance with *dharma*. The best loved are Krishna and Rama (*avatars* of Vishnu).

Krishna is worshipped as a child, as the god of erotic mystical love, and as the hero of the epic *Mahabharata*. While the youthful Krishna with his flute entrances the world with his play (*Krishna-lila*), in the *Bhagavad Gita* Krishna reveals himself as the great teacher and supreme god (Vishnu).

Rama is worshipped as the ideal ruler and the restorer of *dharma*. Always popular in northern India, Rama, has latterly become the principal god of Hindu nationalism. His reign (*Ram Rajya*) is invoked as a golden period of justice, harmony, and prosperity.

IMAGE WORSHIP

While many Hindus acknowledge that *Brahman* is the ultimate reality, the vast majority also worship divine beings and images. Many believe that the power (*shakti*) of a deity is actually present in that deity's image (*murti*). Therefore, in worshipping before an image, worship is offered to the deity whose power is in the image, and also to the deity as an image. When an image is consecrated, the ceremony transforms images of stone, metal, and wood into embodiments of God. Hindus go to the temple for *darshana*, the 'sight' or 'vision' of the deities. It is believed that *darshana* brings good fortune, grace, and spiritual merit. It also makes possible an intimate, loving relationship between deities and their devotees. During ritual worship (*puja*), the gods are served and cared for as honoured guests by the offerings made to their images.

DHARMA

Hindus today often refer to Hindu beliefs and practices as *sanatana dharma* (eternal religion), or Vedic *dharma* (Vedic religion). *Dharma* may mean the social order, or the cosmic order, but equally it can refer to personal behaviour and attitudes. At the simplest level, it means the individual's religious and social duties, according to status and stage of life. The *Bhagavad Gita*, for example, teaches that it is better to do one's own duty imperfectly than that of another well.

SAMSARA

Many Hindus, particularly those in the higher castes, believe in the endless cycle of rebirth (*samsara*). Efforts to bring the cycle to an end are at the core of many Hindu religious practices. The picture of a world as a place where the eternal soul is perpetually reincarnated has dominated the Indian imagination for over three millennia.

KARMA

Central to the teaching about reincarnation, *karma* is the taken-for-granted belief that one's actions determine one's condition in this life and rebirth in the next. Every action has its inevitable fruit or consequence. *Karma* is thus inseparable from *dharma* and *samsara*. To summarize the belief: good deeds result in good *karma*, which produces good fortune in this life and a good birth in the next life; bad deeds result in bad *karma*, which may lead to much less desirable rebirths in the next life, as a human lower down the social hierarchy, as an animal, or even as an unfortunate soul suffering the torments of one of the many hells.

> To see the universal and all-pervading Spirit of Truth face to face one must be able to love the meanest of creation as oneself.
>
> Mahatma Gandhi, *An Autobiography* (Harmondsworth: Penguin, 1982).

There are ways in which *karma* may be overridden. Devotion to a deity is perhaps the most potent, whilst religious rituals and meritorious action may also cancel past sins. Some Hindus withdraw from the world and practise non-engagement. However, the *Bhagavad Gita* teaches that adherence to one's duty, combined with internal renunciation of attachment to, or desire for, the results of one's actions, can lead to liberation (*moksha*) from the cycle of *samsara*.

Karma can lead to either fatalism or ethical activism. It can be seen as an uncontrollable, impersonal determinant of the human condition; or can encourage people to feel responsible for their own fate, and promote a dynamic view of action in the world.

THE THREE PATHS

The three paths — *margas* or *yogas* — to spiritual fulfilment are: *jnana* (knowledge, insight, wisdom), *karma* (action) and *bhakti* (ecstatic devotion). Some Hindus consider each of the three paths requires exclusive concentration, and is sufficient for liberation. However, many modern teachers and gurus teach a *yoga* of synthesis, arguing that the three paths are linked, and liberating knowledge may be obtained through all.

Jnanayoga – the path of wisdom/knowledge – liberates from *karma* and rebirth, and indeed from sickness, old age, and death. It leads to the overcoming of ignorance and the realization of *Brahman*. The pursuit of wisdom implies religious practice, meditation, self-purification, and above all study of the scriptures. The Vedas, and particularly the *Upanishads*, provide knowledge of *Brahman*, and of our true condition. Indeed, the famous teaching of the *Upanishads* is that in soul (*atman*) humans are identical with *Brahman*. According to some Hindu schools, if humans realize this truth, they can be liberated-in-life (*jivan-mukta*).

Karmayoga – the path of work – enables ordinary people everywhere to give spiritual meaning to their everyday lives. It is associated for many with the *Bhagavad Gita's* teaching that action can be a positive means of personal transformation, if people perform their duty selflessly, and act without the desire for status or reward. Gandhi reinterpreted *karmayoga*, by equating

A Hindu pilgrim sits beside the River Ganges, Varanasi, India.

it with social commitment and struggle, and found in the *Gita* authority for his philosophy of non-violence and peaceful resistance to British rule.

Bhaktiyoga – the path of loving devotion – is characterized by an intense personal relationship between the deity and devotee. Selfless love of God consumes past *karma,* and results in a state of intimate, blissful, and loving communion with the deity. Vaishnavas often speak of *prapatti* – complete self-surrender in love – to Vishnu. God-intoxicated saints are depicted as immersed in blissful devotion. Today many busy Hindus follow the path of *bhakti*: their spiritual discipline (*sadhana*) may vary, but is broadly characterized by selfless service and loving devotion to God.

THE FOUR GOALS

Hinduism offers four legitimate goals (*purusartha*) for human beings which, taken together, are believed to ensure spiritual and social harmony:

1. *Artha* – worldly wealth and success – is a proper goal, if pursued without desire, anger, and greed. Kautilya's *Artha Shastra*, written in the third to fourth century BCE, argues that prosperity is the basis of a well-ordered state, and people need *artha* if

they are to practise religion. Thus pursuing an occupation, accumulating wealth, governing and so on are justified if they do not violate *dharma*.

2. *Kama* – pleasure, desire – is also a legitimate goal, if it accords with *dharma*. This is the pursuit of pleasurable activities, including sexuality, play, recreation, the arts, and literature. The *Kama Sutra*, written in the third or fourth centuries CE, deals at length with erotic techniques, the arts of pleasure, and seduction.

3. *Dharma* – virtue, morality – has two levels: it is both one's own particular set of duties (*svadharma*) and the absolute morality, valid universally. When profit and pleasure are pursued for themselves, outside of *dharma*, they lead to social chaos.

4. *Moksha* – spiritual liberation – is the ultimate Hindu quest: release from the bondage of suffering and rebirth (*samsara*).

Some Hindus believe these goals are interconnected and that no goal is primary. Others believe they form an ascending hierarchy, with *moksha* transcending – even opposing – the other three. Whatever one's understanding, this system of the four goals implicitly recognizes the complexity of human drives and aspirations.

> *Just as a person casts off worn-out garments and puts on others that are new, even so the embodied soul casts off worn-out bodies and takes on others that are new. Weapons do not cleave the Self, fire does not burn the Self. Waters do not drench the Self, winds do not parch the Self. The Self is the same forever: unmanifest, unthinkable, still.*
>
> Bhagavad Gita II, 22–25

DEATH AND THE AFTERLIFE

Hindu beliefs about the afterlife are complex. Most Hindus believe they will be reborn into another body, according to their *karma*. However, *moksha* – salvation or ultimate spiritual fulfilment – may be understood in different ways: as final union with *Brahman*; as a perfectly blissful state; as communion with God; or as liberation in some heavenly realm or paradise. Many Hindus may find the concept of salvation, or liberation after death, a very distant ideal.

Moreover, ancient understandings of the afterlife persist, and Vedic views are implied in the death ritual. Funerary rites of passage, and memorial rituals for the dead, indicate a belief in the continued existence of ancestors (*pitr*), who are benefited and pleased by offerings made by their descendants. There are also popular beliefs about the journey of the soul after death; the multiplicity of heavens and hells, and the role of the god of death (Yamraj or Dharmaraj) as judge; and restless or malicious ghosts (*pret*, *bhuta*) who may possess or disturb the living.

TIME

Hindu, Buddhist, and Jain beliefs about the vastness of time, and the age of the universe, in some senses coincide with modern scientific understanding. The classical Hindu view is of gradually deteriorating conditions, until finally the world is destroyed by fire and returns to chaos. The world itself perpetually undergoes cycles of evolution, from a state of non-differentiation, through a series of ages, to its dissolution (*pralaya*) back into the unevolved state, from which the cycle starts again. This process of evolution and dissolution is a 'day of Brahma': each day of Brahma divides into the fourteen 'periods of the Manu'; each of the fourteen periods of Manu divides into four great ages; each of the four great ages divides into four *yugas*. The passing of the *yugas* is marked by progressive moral and physical deterioration. We are now in the middle of the last, and worst, age: the *Kaliyuga*. Hence, that there is apparent moral decline, suffering, famine, and war is no surprise to Hindus; indeed, the orthodox view is that life will get worse as we progress through the *yuga*.

GURUS

The *guru* – spiritual teacher – is a figure of the greatest importance in Hinduism, the object of *darshan* and worship, and comes in all shapes and sizes, traditions and orders. Some may assert their status by virtue of their charisma, others are initiated into a long-established lineage (*sampradaya*). Many have carried their spiritual message to the West, helping to extend the bounds of Hinduism. One of the best known gurus was Sathya Sai Baba, worshipped as an *avatara* of Sirdi Sai Baba, and of Shiva and Shakti. There have also been women gurus, such as Sarada Devi (1853–1920), widow of Ramakrishna, Mira Alfassa (1878–1973), Mother of the Aurobindo organization, Ananda Mayi Ma (1896–1982), and Mata Amritanandamayi (b. 1953).

ANNA S. KING

CHAPTER 13

Worship and Festivals

YAJNA

In early Vedic times, worship usually took the form of a sacrificial ritual (*yajna*), addressed to nature gods such as the sun god, Surya; the rain god, Indra; the god of fire, Agni; or the Soma god, believed to reside in a probably hallucinogenic plant of the same name. These rituals involved the sacrifice of animals such as goats and cows, or the pouring of oblations of such items as clarified butter, honey, and milk into a sacrificial fire, accompanied by the chanting of Vedic hymns and prayers. The early Vedas are liturgical texts, which set out in great detail the method of ritual observance. These rituals were intended to please the gods through worship, and to ensure the well-being of the sponsor or patron of the sacrifice – the *yajamana* – and his family.

PUJA

Yajnas are something of a rarity in the contemporary Hindu world; far more commonly observed is *puja*, a ritual of devotional worship regularly conducted at temples, usually by Brahman priests, and often observed privately at household shrines. *Puja* may be addressed to any of the manifold gods and goddesses in the Hindu pantheon, important among whom are the great gods Vishnu and Shiva, and the goddess Shakti, all of whom appear in myriad forms and aspects in Hindu mythology, and across the contemporary Hindu sacred landscape.

> *Whatever you do, or eat, or give, or offer in adoration, let it be an offering to me; and whatever you suffer, suffer it for me.*
>
> Bhagavad Gita 9.26

Temples dedicated to the different Hindu gods and goddesses usually contain a sanctified image of the deity, and to this image the ritual of *puja* is addressed. During *puja*, the priest ritually purifies himself and the shrine, invokes the presence of the deity in the image, and then worships the image by ritually bathing and adorning it, feeding it symbolically, and waving a flaming lamp in a circle around it in a ritual of light. This is usually accompanied by the chanting of Sanskrit mantras, the blowing of conches, and the ringing of bells. In Hindu households, the family usually observes an abbreviated form of this ritual.

The relationship between the image and the divine presence is, in the Hindu world, often a complex one. For most Hindus, the image is symbolic of the divine presence; but for many, it is also the divine presence, manifesting itself in tangible form. Moreover, Hindus seldom agree on the importance of *puja*. While some see it as an act of great religious significance, others see it as a largely unnecessary, outward expression of religious piety, and prefer instead a more inward-oriented mode of spiritual development. Besides *puja*, other modes of worship commonly practised in Hindu society include *bhajana* – the singing of hymns – and the recitation of the *sahasranama*, the thousand names of the gods and goddesses.

Part of the huge Hindu temple complex at Angkor Wat, Cambodia – the world's largest religious monument – built by the Tamil king Suryavarnman II in the twelfth century CE.

I am the same to all beings, and my love is ever the same; but those who worship me with devotion, they are in me and I am in them.

Bhagavad Gita 9.29

A BRIEF INTRODUCTION TO HINDUISM

Festivals of Hinduism

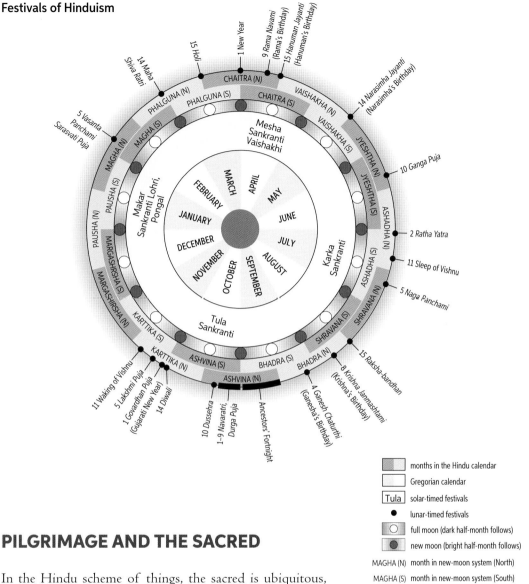

months in the Hindu calendar

Gregorian calendar

Tula   solar-timed festivals

●   lunar-timed festivals

○   full moon (dark half-month follows)

◐   new moon (bright half-month follows)

MAGHA (N)   month in new-moon system (North)

MAGHA (S)   month in new-moon system (South)

PILGRIMAGE AND THE SACRED

In the Hindu scheme of things, the sacred is ubiquitous, contained not only in temples and sacred images, but also in nature — in stones, trees, mountains, and rivers. Every once in a while the sacred 'manifests' itself in the form of a mysterious rock, stream, or spring, and the site of such manifestation becomes a place of worship. Pilgrims flock to such places during auspicious months of the Hindu calendar, and mythological stories grow about the miraculous nature of the pilgrimage site. Particularly important in the Hindu cosmology are sacred rivers, and holy towns and cities situated along their banks, which are seen as places of crossing (*tirtha*) between the mundane and the sacred, and between the worlds of the living and the dead. The water of the Ganges in North

Hindu pilgrims gather on the banks of the holy River Ganges at Varanasi, India, to perform their morning religious rituals.

A BRIEF INTRODUCTION TO HINDUISM

India is believed to be especially potent in this respect, and a single dip in the river is believed to earn for the worshipper untold spiritual merit.

The sacred often manifests itself in living things too. The cow, the monkey, and – in some parts of India – even the snake and the rat are believed to be sacred and therefore worshipped. Yet more common is the worship of men and women believed to be holy, and therefore capable of performing miracles that can transform the lives of devotees, and ensure their well-being. Many such holy figures attract an extensive following, and head vast spiritual empires extending across regional and national boundaries.

FESTIVALS

The Hindu (lunar) calendar year is punctuated by a series of religious festivals. Temple festivals are usually marked by processions, when worshippers carry the deity's image through the temple town or village, offering devotees a chance to glimpse it in all its glory. Other festivals – which celebrate landmark events in Hindu mythology – include:

Image of Durga, a popular fierce form of the Hindu goddess, depicted with up to eighteen arms.

- *Janmashtami* (July–August): the celebration of the birthday of the popular Hindu god, Krishna.
- *Ganesh Chaturthi* (August–September): a festival dedicated to the elephant-headed god, Ganesh, the remover of obstacles.
- *Dussehra* (September–October, towards the end of the monsoon): marking the victory of Rama and his monkey army over the demon-king Ravana. It encompasses *Navaratri* – also known as 'the festival of nine nights' – which in Bengal culminates in a grand celebration dedicated to the worship of the goddess Durga.
- *Diwali* (October–November): the festival of lights, following shortly after *Dussehra*. Hindus throughout the world illuminate their homes with lamps and exchange gifts.

- *Shivaratri* (January–February): a festival during which Shiva is worshipped.
- *Holi* (February–March): a spring festival, during which people drench one another in water and coloured powder.

Besides these, there are several localized festivals observed in different parts of the Hindu world. The *Kumbh Mela*, perhaps the most popular of these, attracts pilgrims in vast numbers to its four sites in North India – Hardwar, Nasik, Ujjain, and Allahabad – where it is celebrated on a rotational basis once every three years. The *Purna Kumbha Mela* takes place once every twelve years in the holy town of Allahabad. Billed as the 'biggest gathering on earth', in 2001 more than 40 million people gathered on its busiest days.

MAYA WARRIER

CHAPTER 14

Family and Society

Caste and joint family are often seen as the central features of traditional Hindu social organization. The caste system orders Hindu society hierarchically, such that different social groups are ranked in a relationship of superiority or inferiority to each other in terms of their levels of purity. Every Hindu is born into the caste of his or her parents. Traditionally, caste groups were — by and large — occupational groups, and the nature of one's occupation determined one's level of purity. Ritual, worship, and scholarship in sacred texts, seen as the purest pursuits, were the preserve of the 'purest' and 'highest' of castes, the Brahmans. At the opposite end of the hierarchy were the so-called 'untouchables', who, by virtue of the 'impurity' attaching to their occupations — scavenging, tanning leather and the like — were considered too polluting to be incorporated into mainstream society, and were therefore excluded from everyday social life. Between these two extremes ranged a vast and varied spectrum of caste rankings. In traditional Indian village society, caste determined most aspects of one's life — where one lived, with whom one could legitimately interact, with whom one could share food, and whom one could marry. As a result, social mobility, especially for those on the lowest rungs of society, was highly restricted.

THE JOINT FAMILY

Just as caste determined one's place in society, so status within the joint family determined one's place within the household. In the joint family system, two, often three, or even four generations of a family lived together, as part of the same household, sharing common living space and kitchen facilities, drawing from a common pool of financial resources, and sharing responsibilities for the upkeep of the family home. The head of the household was usually the oldest male member of the family. In the traditional Hindu family system, family property passed down the male line; the women of the family seldom owned or controlled family property. Indian epic narratives, such as the *Mahabharata* and *Ramayana*, dwell at great length on familial roles and duties as

> For the sake of the family, one may abandon an individual. For the sake of a village one may abandon a family. For the country's sake, one may abandon a village. For the sake of the soul, one may abandon the world!
>
> Mahabharata 2.55.10

husband, wife, father, mother, son, daughter, brother and so on, thus providing traditional models for good conduct in familial contexts.

MARRIAGE

Traditionally, a woman derived her identity from the male authority figures in her life: usually her father before her marriage, her husband after marriage, and her sons in her old age. Marriage was – and remains to this day – a central institution, ordering and regulating the Hindu social system. Conventionally, marriage is seen, not as the formalizing of a romantic relationship between the individuals concerned, but as an arrangement between families of the same, or similarly ranked, caste groups within the caste hierarchy. The bride, seen in most Hindu communities as a 'gift' from her parents to the family of the

I AM A HINDU

I was born a few years after India gained independence, in a village in Gujarat, India, just outside the town of Dandi – famous for Gandhi's Salt March protest against the British colonial government. I came to England when I was eleven, because my father was employed in a car factory in Coventry. Although I attended school in India from the age of five, I found schooling in England difficult, mainly because I knew little English. However, I quickly learned the new language and settled in.

At sixteen, I joined a local engineering company, and began an apprenticeship. After five years, I successfully concluded it, and was encouraged to apply to Sussex University. After being awarded a degree in Mechanical Engineering, I returned to the company, and worked my way up to become one of their chief engineers, which has led to my travelling to various parts of the world.

As a Hindu, I believe in one God who has many incarnations (*avatars*). I believe in all these gods, but – like many Hindus – focus on a particular god who has become special to me: Krishna, a very popular god within Hinduism. I am particularly moved and helped by the many stories about Krishna. My belief in God has encouraged me to be a helpful, contributing member of society. For instance, I assisted in starting a cricket

club for young people, and I have been its secretary for thirty years. I did this because, as a Hindu, I wanted to put something back into the community from which I have benefited so much. I believe that, if I lead a good life, helping others, and worshipping God, as a result of reincarnation I will be reborn into a better life.

I do not believe it is necessary to visit the temple every day to keep in touch with God. God is with me every hour of the day. I pray to God in my thoughts wherever I am, and reflect on my beliefs, and whether what I'm doing is good for me or for other people. I do this, not only because they are good things to do, but also because they will contribute to a good reincarnation. That said, I like to be in the temple whenever I can, serving my community. I find that regular attendance helps my religious life, by expanding my thoughts, and helping to make me less selfish and to see the best in others. This is what faith means to me. It is a faith I learned particularly from my mother, a traditional Hindu; she has been the greatest influence on my religious upbringing.

When we moved to Cheltenham, we were the first Hindu family, and there was no temple. We had a shrine in our house, but had to return to Coventry for important festivals, celebrating there as we had done in India, if on a smaller scale. Finally, in 1975, the growing groom, often brings wealth – in the form of dowry – to the groom's family. Her parents, in popular belief, derive spiritual merit by gifting their daughter to the groom's family. Although in some instances it is permissible for the woman to 'marry up' into a family of higher social standing than her own, the reverse, where the woman marries someone from a lower caste, is considered taboo.

FAMILY AND SOCIETY TODAY

While the institutions of caste and joint family still prevail in contemporary Hindu society, they have undergone vast changes, mainly due to changes in economic organization. The status of women in society too has undergone some measure of change, although several traditional ideas regarding the woman's role in the family still prevail. In modern

Hindu community in Cheltenham established their own temple, an occasion of much rejoicing and celebration.

In 1976 I returned to India, where I met my wife, a traditional Hindu from Gujarat. Already a devout Hindu, after our marriage I became more involved in the activities of the temple, as its secretary and now its treasurer. Because of my work, I do not participate in worship in the temple every day, but attend at least three times a week. When I retire, I will attend worship in the temple far more regularly.

In our home, we have a temple-like shrine, at which my mother and my wife perform *puja* every day. After bathing in the morning, I also pray there for a short time. I observe fasting on special occasions, but am not too particular about my diet. My wife and my mother are far more traditionally Hindu in this respect. My faith is more interior than exterior: I am less concerned about outward symbols, such as dress, than I am about what I think and do. That said, I do often wear traditional Indian dress for *puja* and other religious functions.

I do not have time to attend scripture study regularly. Once or twice a year I attend scripture reading and exposition in Coventry. I would like to go regularly to a local reading of Hindu sacred texts, but none is available, although scholars from the Hare Krishna

temple in Watford are sometimes invited to explain Hindu texts locally.

I visit India most years, and whenever I go I make a point of visiting places of pilgrimage or particular temples. My aspiration is to visit most of the temples and sacred places in South India, which I believe are the original Hindu temples. My goal, when I retire, is to devote my life to seeking inner peace through prayer and meditation.

My wife is more devout than I am, and observes all the Hindu calendar events, and my family life is firmly based on Hindu religion and culture. My faith has helped strengthen my relationship with my wife, mother, and sisters. Together we observe all the Hindu festivals and celebrations, such as *Navaratri* and *Janmashtami*, and key ceremonies (*samskars*) such as cyclical funerary rites (*sraddha*). I took my father's ashes to India to scatter in rivers and on the land, especially in our hometown.

As a Hindu community we are very close-knit. We all get to know about the sickness, death, and other problems faced by other Hindu families. The close friendships we have mean we are always ready to support each other in times of need.

Naren Patel

Hindu society, one's caste need no longer determine one's occupation, income, or social status. Particularly in urban contexts, where modern occupations and workplaces afford employees some degree of autonomy from caste restrictions, caste often ceases to be the all-important marker of one's identity. The joint family system likewise worked best when occupations were hereditary, and different generations of a family derived their income from the same source of livelihood. With urbanization and industrialization generating new, and more numerous, job opportunities, and modern educational institutions imparting new skills to recruits from diverse backgrounds, it has been possible for younger generations not only to break away from their hereditary familial occupations and move into new kinds of employment, but also to set up independent nuclear families of their own. With more and more women entering educational institutions and the employment sector, they too need less support from the male members of their families. They are thus, to some degree, able to assert their independence and autonomy from the traditional family structure.

While in several instances the nuclear family has come to replace the joint family, the idea of the joint family retains a powerful hold over the Hindu imagination. Families tend to be closely networked across generations, and older members of the family, although they may not live in close proximity to younger members, continue to exercise considerable authority over the latter. Parents still have a major say in determining same-caste life partners for their sons and daughters, even though the concept of the 'love marriage' as opposed to the 'arranged marriage' is gaining increasing popularity in the contemporary Hindu world. Families come together on occasions such as birth, wedding, and death ceremonies, reinforcing a sense of solidarity as a group. Hindu epic stories, such as the *Mahabharata* and *Ramayana*, are often retold today in the form of television serials and dance dramas, bolstering the ideal of the joint family in popular thinking.

MAYA WARRIER

CHAPTER 15

Hinduism in the Modern World

Hinduism, the most ancient world religion, has been subject to many changes in the course of its long history. The rise and fall in prominence of some ancient gods, such as Indra, King of gods, and Varuna, god of the sea; the decline in importance of the fire sacrifice; the rise in popularity of the *bhakti* (devotional) tradition in the sixth century CE are all instances of this. In the nineteenth and early twentieth centuries Hindu reformers such as Vivekananda (1863–1902), Ram Mohan Roy (1772–1833), Mohandas (Mahatma) Gandhi (1869–1948), and Sarvepalli Radhakrishnan (1888–1975) advocated an ethical form of Hinduism, which campaigned against social practices such as *sati* – the self-immolation of widows on their husbands' funeral pyres – and child marriage, and displayed the influence of Western values. In modern times, Hinduism has moved away from this puritanical type of religion, which decried many ancient beliefs as superstitious, and has returned with full vigour to traditional Hinduism.

ASTROLOGERS AND GURUS

A large number of Hindus now defend traditional Hindu mores and practices. Contemporary Hindus are not worried about being labelled 'superstitious', and openly consult astrologers and gurus. The increased veneration of gurus has given rise to the cult phenomenon in modern Hinduism. Some prominent gurus, such as Swami Prabhupada, Bhagavan Rajneesh, and Satya Sai Baba, established popular new religious movements that have spread beyond India, attracting a considerable following from Westerners, although, technically, conversion into Hinduism is impossible, because Hindus are – as a result of their *karma* – those born into Hindu families and into a particular caste. Non-Hindus do not have a caste identity; hence, traditionally Hindu missionary activity was aimed at recovering Hindus who had lapsed into Christianity or Islam, and required a purification ritual, or *shuddi*. However, in the modern world, new cults and movements have emulated Christians, by engaging in mission to non-Hindus. Many of these new Hindu movements have been successful in recruiting Westerners.

POLITICIZATION

One of the most striking modern developments has been the politicization of Hinduism, and the rising militancy among some factions, perhaps a natural consequence of the emergence of Hindu nationalism in a country so long under the yoke of Muslim and Christian powers. Independence for India in August 1947 ended around 400 years of such rule and, although the Indian leaders opted for a secular, or religiously neutral, nation, the vast majority of the population is Hindu. With the passing of time, the secular ideals of Jawaharlal Nehru (1889–1964) – first Prime Minister of India – and Gandhi have become less valued, and today many view India as a Hindu, rather than a secular, multi-religious, nation.

This shift toward Hindu nationalism should be seen in the context of the rise of Muslim nationalism in the subcontinent, and the perennial dispute over Kashmir, the Muslim-majority state located between India and Pakistan. Hindu nationalistic parties such as the RSS (Rashtriya Swayam Sevak Sangh/National Self-Service Association), the VHP (Vishwa Hindu Parishad/World Hindu Organization) and BJP (Bharatiya Janatha Party/Indian People's Party) promote India as a Hindu

The Birla Mandir, or Laxmi Narayan, Hindu Temple, Delhi, India, built between 1933 and 1939.

A BRIEF INTRODUCTION TO HINDUISM

state, and believe Hindu religion, ideology, and values should predominate. This has increased pressure on the religious minorities and created division. The actions and claims of more militant sections of Hindu nationalist organizations, such as the Bajrang Dal, have been denounced by Hindu intellectuals as uncharacteristic of Hindu religion and culture, with its image of tolerance, and willingness to absorb beliefs and practices from other religions and philosophies. The militants have an ideology based on *Hindutva* ('Hindu-ness'), which raises problems for the religious minorities, and raises the possibility of a Hindu theocratic state, alienating the millions of non-Hindus in the nation.

The appeal of the Hindu nationalistic ideology is more evident among the less literate and rural sections of the Hindu community, who constitute the majority of the Indian populace. This combination of political power and militant religious nationalism has led to tension in some areas of India where several faith communities live alongside each other. The massacre of Muslims in Gujarat in 2002 was allegedly condoned, and even abetted, by the Hindu nationalist state government. Hindu nationalists seek the Hinduization of Indian polity, culture, and education. This trend, often termed 'saffronization' — saffron being a colour associated with Hinduism — is growing stronger, although opposed by the Indian intelligentsia, who argue against the politicization of religion, its identification with the nation and growing hostility to other faiths.

THE HINDU DIASPORA

A significant development in Hinduism has resulted from the migration of many Hindus to the West. Because these diaspora communities are minorities, a defensive, more fervent type of Hinduism has emerged. For example, in southern states of the USA, where there is a strong conservative Christian culture, Hindus have challenged what they see as the misrepresentation of Hindu concepts and practices in school textbooks.

Westernized Hindu ideas, when imported back to India, have been responsible for an increased awareness of mystical traditions, sacred sites, and some esoteric forms of Hindu spirituality. There has been a burgeoning interest in pilgrimage to sacred shrines, such as the Sabarimala Temple in Kerala, and great festivals, such as the *Kumbh Mela*. There has also been an increase in pilgrims visiting gurus in search of miracles.

THE CASTE SYSTEM

Modern Hinduism has also seen a strengthening of the caste system. At the turn of the twentieth century, a campaign by Hindu reformers such as Dayananda Sarasvati (1824–83), Vivekananda, and Gandhi sought to reform what they saw as the chauvinism and discrimination of the caste system. Caste did not disappear, but it was felt to be out of date and incompatible with modern egalitarian ideals. For some, the conversion of 'untouchables' to Christianity, Islam, or Buddhism seemed to threaten the predominance of Hinduism in the subcontinent. Under Gandhi's influence, the Indian constitution and laws guaranteed privileges to the untouchables in education and employment. In recent years this has faced opposition by 'forward communities', who claim positive discrimination policies have undermined the economic status of their own communities. In some areas there have been caste wars between the *savarnas* – those belonging to the *varna* or caste system – and the *avarnas* – the untouchables. Both the untouchables and the *savarnas* have now organized into vote banks to achieve political influence.

Revisionist thinking now emphasizes the positive side of the caste system. Even practices such as *sati* have been praised by fundamentalists, despite a growing feminist movement within Hinduism. On the other hand, there is a phenomenon termed 'sanskritization', which has seen untouchables and tribal peoples of India attempting to Hinduize their religious practices. Some untouchable and tribal groups are beginning to abandon their traditional deities and practices to build temples and worship Hindu deities, such as Vishnu and Shiva, possibly in an attempt to enter the Hindu fold, or gain higher status for their community. The Indian constitution has made the restriction of entry of untouchables to Hindu temples illegal, and some untouchables have undertaken Hindu theological training and demanded entry to the priesthood, even at *savarna* temples.

Meanwhile, other untouchable and tribal groups have retained their traditional pantheon and ritual praxis, but attempted to identify their deities and practices with Hindu gods and worship, by reinterpreting their mythology and ritual proceedings. The leaders of the Muthappan cult of northern Kerala, for example, have reinterpreted the Muthappan deities as Vishnu and Shiva, although originally tribal gods of the forest dwellers of the region.

WOMEN IN MODERN HINDUISM

Nineteenth-century and twentieth-century social reformers spearheaded efforts to achieve the liberation of women, at considerable risk. Ram Mohan Roy's campaign resulted in the banning of *sati*. Ishwar Chandra Vidyasagar married a widow, to set an example of improving the lot of people treated as virtually dead – widows lived in seclusion, were not allowed to remarry, had to forgo all adornments, and were looked on as inauspicious. Gandhi, for the first time in modern India, brought Indian women into the public arena, in his campaign for independence. Women took part in public demonstrations and in the civil disobedience movement. The momentum gained has not been lost: the traditional image of the Hindu woman – domesticated and subservient to father and husband – is changing rapidly. Women are well represented in the employment sector and in government, and there has been a move to set quotas for women members of the *Lok Sabha* (parliament). A Vanitha Commission (Woman's Commission) in Kerala State is looking into women's grievances, including molestation or 'eve teasing' in public places, discrimination in employment, and their position in the family.

Traditionally, the role of the woman was in the home, serving her husband and nurturing her children. Hindu mythology often emphasized this image. Female figures such as Sita, the virtuous and long suffering wife of Rama, and Savithri, who pleaded successfully to

Yama, the god of death, for the life of her husband, were held up as paradigms of womanly behaviour. Modern Hindu women do not adhere to these norms; they are out in public, competing against men in all fields, even in occupations traditionally viewed as exclusively male, such as law, engineering, and the police and armed forces. Feminist groups such as the Working Woman's Forum are active in trying to achieve equality. Film directors such as Mira Nair and Deepa Mehta have made films highlighting the aspirations of Indian women and the problems they face, such as *Fire* (1996) and *Monsoon Wedding* (2001), provoking controversy among right-wing Hindu groups.

THEODORE GABRIEL

QUESTIONS

1. What continuities are there between early Vedic religion and modern Hinduism?

2. Explain the different views of the role of *Brahman* in Hinduism.

3. Explain the different views of the nature of human existence held by the three main Vedantic schools (*Advaita*, *Vishishtadvaita*, and *Dvaita*).

4. What role do the *Ramayana* and *Mahabarata* play in helping to attain liberation?

5. Explain why some believe the term 'Hinduisms' to be more appropriate than 'Hinduism'.

6. Why are Shiva and Vishnu considered to be so important?

7. Why do Hindus understand *moksha* (liberation) in a variety of different ways?

8. Explain some of the different roles of the guru in Hinduism.

9. Why are some geographical sites seen as sacred in Hinduism?

10. Why has the caste system been so important in Hinduism and Indian society?

FURTHER READING

Biardeau, Madeleine, *Hinduism: The Anthropology of a Civilization*. Delhi: Oxford University Press, 1989.

Blurton, T. Richard, *Hindu Art*. Cambridge: Harvard University Press, 1992.

Hiriyanna, Mysore, *The Essentials of Indian Philosophy*. London: Allen and Unwin, 1985.

Kinsley, David R., *Hindu Goddesses: Visions of the Divine Feminine in the Hindu Religious Tradition*. Berkeley: University of California Press, 1988.

Lopez, Donald S. Jr., ed., *Religions of India in Practice*. Princeton: Princeton University Press, 1995.

Mittal, S., and G. Thursby, eds., *The Hindu World*. New York: Routledge, 2004.

Narayan, R. K., *Ramayana: A Shortened Modern Prose Version of the Indian Epic*. New York: Viking, 1972.

Swami Prabhavananda and Frederick Manchester, trans., *The Upanishads*. New York: Signet, 2002.

Swami Prabhavananda and Christopher Isherwood, trans., *Bhagavad-Gita: The Song of God*. New York: Signet, 2002.

von Stietencron, Heinrich, 'Hinduism: On the Proper Use of a Deceptive Term', in Gunther D. Sontheimer and Hermann Kulke, eds., *Hinduism Reconsidered*, pp. 11–27. New Delhi: Manohar, 1989.

Williams, Raymond Brady, ed., *A Sacred Thread: Modern Transmission of Hindu Traditions in India and Abroad*. Chambersburg, PA: Anima, 1992.

GALLERY

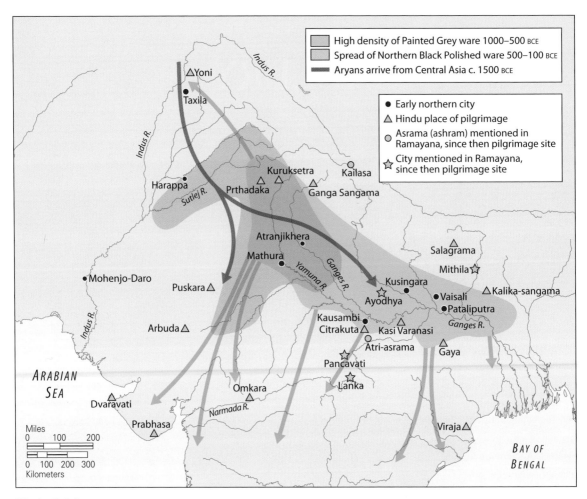

Legend

- High density of Painted Grey ware 1000–500 BCE
- Spread of Northern Black Polished ware 500–100 BCE
- Aryans arrive from Central Asia c. 1500 BCE

- ● Early northern city
- △ Hindu place of pilgrimage
- ○ Asrama (ashram) mentioned in Ramayana, since then pilgrimage site
- ☆ City mentioned in Ramayana, since then pilgrimage site

Indus R.

△ Yoni
● Taxila

● Harappa
Sutlej R.
Prthadaka
△ Kuruksetra △
Ganga Sangama △
○ Kailasa

Indus R.

Atranjikhera
Mathura ●
Yamuna R.
Ganges R.
△ Salagrama
Mithila ☆

● Mohenjo-Daro
Puskara △
Kusingara ●
Ayodhya ☆
Vaisali ●
Pataliputra ●
△ Kalika-sangama

Arbuda △
Kausambi ●
Citrakuta △
Atri-asrama ○
Kasi Varanasi △
Ganges R.
Gaya △

Pancavati ☆

ARABIAN
SEA
Lanka ☆
Omkara △
Dvaravati △
Prabhasa △
Narmada R.
Viraja △

Miles
0   100   200

0 100 200 300
Kilometers

BAY OF
BENGAL

Hindu Origins

Indian sadhu near the Ganges river at
Haridwar, Uttarakhand, India.

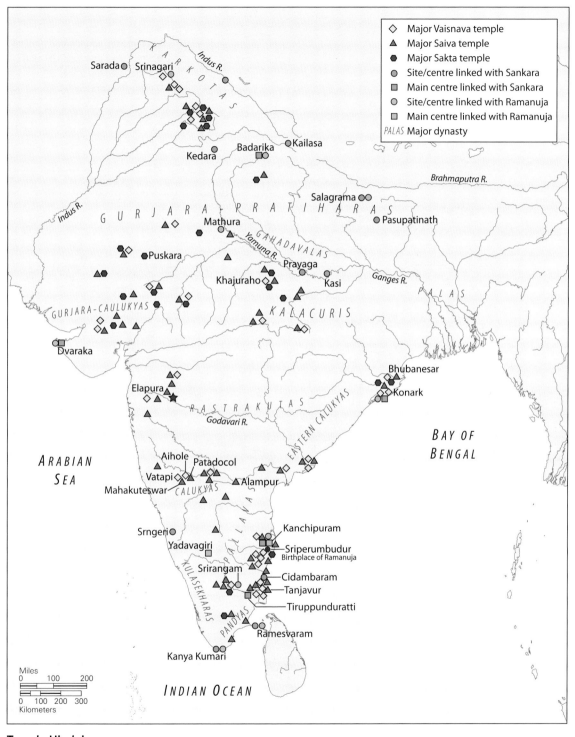

Temple Hinduism

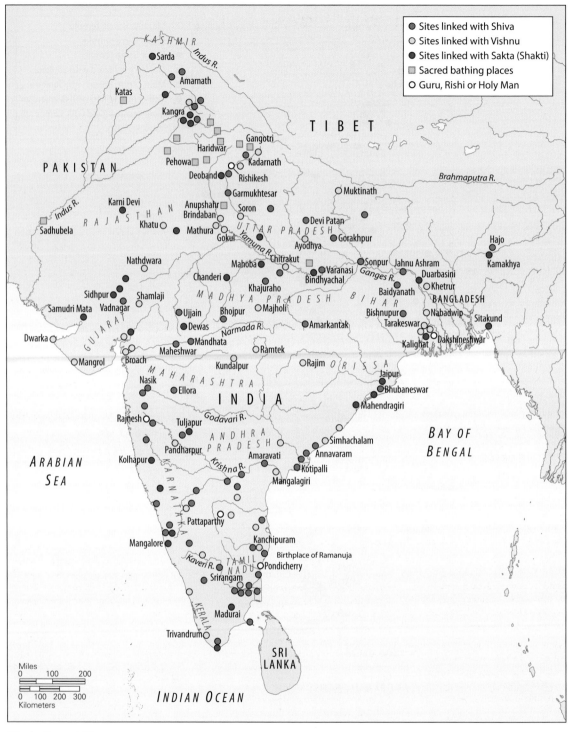

Legend:
- Sites linked with Shiva
- Sites linked with Vishnu
- Sites linked with Sakta (Shakti)
- Sacred bathing places
- Guru, Rishi or Holy Man

Labels on map:

KASHMIR
Sarda
Indus R.
Amarnath
Katas
Kangra
TIBET
Gangotri
Haridwar
Kadarnath
Brahmaputra R.
PAKISTAN
Pehowa
Deoband
Rishikesh
Garmukhtesar
Muktinath
Karni Devi
Anupshahr
Brindaban
Soron
Devi Patan
Hajo
Indus R.
RAJASTHAN
Khatu
Mathura
Gokul
UTTAR PRADESH
Gorakhpur
Kamakhya
Sadhubela
Yamuna R.
Ayodhya
Nathdwara
Chitrakut
Sonpur
Jahnu Ashram
Mahoba
Duarbasini
Sidhpur
Chanderi
Khajuraho
Varanasi
Baidyanath
Khetrur
Shamlaji
MADHYA PRADESH
Bindhyachal
BIHAR
BANGLADESH
Samudri Mata
Vadnagar
Ujjain
Bhojpur
Majholi
Bishnupur
Nabadwip
Sitakund
Dewas
Narmada R.
Amarkantak
Tarakeswar
Dwarka
GUJARAT
Mandhata
Maheshwar
Ramtek
Kalighat
Dakshineshwar
Mangrol
Broach
Kundalpur
Rajim
ORISSA
Nasik
MAHARASHTRA
Jaipur
INDIA
Bhubaneswar
Ellora
Mahendragiri
Rajnesh
Godavari R.
Tuljapur
ANDHRA PRADESH
Simhachalam
ARABIAN SEA
Pandharpur
BAY OF BENGAL
Kolhapur
Amaravati
Annavaram
Krishna R.
Kotipalli
Mangalagiri
Pattaparthy
Kanchipuram
Mangalore
Birthplace of Ramanuja
Kaveri R.
TAMIL NADU
Pondicherry
Srirangam
KERALA
Madurai
Trivandrum
SRI LANKA
INDIAN OCEAN

Miles
0   100   200

0   100   200   300
Kilometers

Hindu Sacred Places

A BRIEF INTRODUCTION TO HINDUISM

Rapid Fact-Finder

A

Absolute, The Term for God or the divine often preferred by those who conceive of God predominantly in abstract or impersonal terms.

Advaita ('non-dualism') The monist (*see* monism) doctrine of Shankara, that all reality is fundamentally one and divine.

Afterlife Any form of conscious existence after the death of the body.

Agni Indian fire god of Vedic times (*see* Vedas). As sacrificial fire, Agni mediates between gods and people and is especially concerned with order and ritual.

Ahimsa Indian virtue of non-violence. It usually applies to abstention from harming any living creature and hence to vegetarianism. The doctrine was developed in Jainism, Buddhism, and some Hindu sects. In Jain belief violence carries severe penalties of karma. Mahatma Gandhi applied the idea to the political struggles of the oppressed in his practice of non-violent non-cooperation.

Animism A term formerly used to describe pre-literary religions. It was dropped because its meaning, 'spiritism', was felt to be misleading

Archetypes Term invented by C. G. Jung to describe the concepts held in common by different people at different times and in different places. He believed that the concept of God was the archetype of the self and that it was the object of each individual to discover it.

Aryan Word describing the Caucasian people who invaded India around 2000 BCE and who gradually imposed their language and culture upon the earlier inhabitants. Related peoples settled in Iran and Mesopotamia.

Asceticism Austere practices designed to lead to the control of the body and the senses. These may include fasting and meditation, the renunciation of possessions, and the pursuit of solitude.

Ashram In Indian religion, a hermitage or monastery. It has come to denote a communal house for devotees of a guru.

It functions as a centre for building up the commitment of believers and for transmitting the guru's message.

Astrology The study of the influence of the stars on the character and destiny of human beings. The locations of the planets in the field of the zodiac at the time of the subject's birth are the key date considered in the astrologer's analysis.

Atman Sanskrit word meaning soul or self. The Upanishads teach that *atman* is identical to brahman, i.e. the soul is one with the divine.

Atonement Ritual act which restores harmony between the human and the divine when it has been broken by sin or impurity.

Austerity Ascetic practice in which one exercises self-restraint or denial, for example, the restriction of food during a fast.

Avatar ('one who descends') In popular Hinduism, Lord Vishnu appears on earth at intervals to assert ancient values and destroy illusion. The main tradition refers to ten descents, nine of which have already happened. Krishna is the most famous *avatar*. Some modern cults claim to worship a living *avatar*.

B

Benares/Varanasi/Kashi The most holy city of Hinduism, situated on the banks of the Ganges. It is a centre for the worship of Shiva and attracts a million pilgrims every year.

Bhagavad Gita ('song of the lord') A section of the Mahabharata in the form of a battlefield dialogue between the warrior prince Arjuna and Krishna, disguised as his charioteer. Arjuna is unwilling to fight his kinsmen but Krishna encourages him, teaching him that wisdom requires him to fulfil his proper role while at the same time renouncing the consequences of his actions.

Bhagavan/Bhagwan Indian title meaning 'lord' or 'worshipful'. It is frequently used of Vishnu. It is also a title of honour used by devotees of holy men.

Bhagavan Shree Rajneesh (1931–90 CE) Indian spiritual teacher and philosopher who founded his own ashram at Pune (Poona) in India. His daily talks and reflections have been transcribed and widely published in the West.

Bhajana An Indian song or hymn in praise of God usually sung communally at devotional gatherings and accompanied by musical instruments.

Bhakti Love of, or devotion to, God. It is one of the Hindu paths to union with God (*see* yoga). It is expressed in popular religion in which the worshipper develops a sense of personal relationship to God, responding to him as though to a father, mother, friend, lover, or child, and looking to him for grace.

Blavatsky, Helena Petrovna (1831–91 CE) Founder in 1875 of the Theosophical Society (*see* Theosophy), who claimed to have received the 'ancient wisdom' after seven years in Tibet being taught by various Mahatmas. She wrote books defending spiritualism and various occult teachings.

Brahma The creator god of Hinduism. With Vishnu and Shiva, Brahma belongs to the Trimurti of classical Hindu thought.

Brahman In Hinduism, the divine, absolute reality.

Brahmins *see* caste system.

C

Caste system The division of a society into groups reflecting and defining the division of labour. In Hinduism, caste is traditionally seen as the creation of Brahma, each caste emerging symbolically from different parts of his body. There are four chief groups (*varnas*): Brahmins, priests, come from Brahma's mouth; Kshatriyas, warriors, come from Brahma's arms; Vaishyas, commoners, come from Brahma's thighs; Sudras, servants, come from Brahma's feet. Groups of no definite caste were regarded as Untouchables and were banished from society.

Chakras According to Indian thought and many contemporary alternative spiritualities, there are seven (sometimes six) chakras (meaning 'wheels') or spiritual energy centres located in the human body. They are: at the top of the head; between the eyebrows; at the throat; at the heart; at the navel; at the genitals; and at the base of the spine, where kundalini, the serpent-energy, lies coiled. The chakras are sometimes called 'lotus centres'.

Chela In Indian religion, a disciple, student, or follower of a guru.

Civil religion Religion as a system of beliefs, symbols, and practices which legitimate the authority of a society's institutions and bind people together in the public sphere.

Conversion A moral or spiritual change of direction, or the adoption of religious beliefs not previously held.

Cosmology (1) The study of the nature of the cosmos. (2) In religion, cosmologies concern the relationship between the divine and the natural world. This relationship is usually described in myths or stories of how God or the gods had brought the world, humanity, and particular peoples into existence and how they continue to relate to them. Cosmologies form the frameworks within which reality is interpreted.

Creation The act of God by which the universe came into being. Hence also refers to the universe itself. In Hinduism it is believed that the universe has been outpoured from God and will contract into him at the end of the age.

Creation myth A story that explains the divine origins of a particular people, a place or the whole world. In some indigenous religions and ancient religions it is ritually re-enacted at the beginning of each year.

D

Dasara An Indian festival usually celebrated in October. Different parts of India celebrate the festival in different ways and focus on different deities. The celebrations vary from a day to nine days to a month. Those who celebrate it as 'Dussehra' worship the goddess Durga or celebrate Rama's victory over Ravana.

Devil Term generally used to describe an evil spirit.

Dharma In Hinduism, cosmic order, the law of existence, right conduct. Also, in Buddhism, the teaching of the Buddha (*see* dhamma).

Diaspora The geographical spread of a people who share a common culture.

Disciple Followers of a religious leader or teaching.

Divali *see* **Diwali**.

Divinities Name given to minor gods or spirits in indigenous religions who rule over an area of the world or some human activity – e.g. storms, war, farming, marriage. Divinities are usually worshipped formally with special rituals and festivals.

Diwali Festival of light celebrated by Hindus, Jains, and Sikhs. For Hindus it marks the return of Rama from exile and his reunion with Sita as told in the Ramayana.

Doctrine A religious teaching or belief which is taught and upheld within a particular religious community.

Dravidian Word describing the pre-Aryan civilization based in the Indus valley. It was overturned by Aryan invaders around 2000 BCE. Today Dravidian peoples inhabit southern India.

Dreams One of the chief sources of revelation to the individual in indigenous religions. Dreams may contain warnings or commands or promises of blessing.

Durga ('the inaccessible') In Hindu tradition, the consort of Shiva in one of her terrifying forms.

E

Esoteric Word meaning 'inner', suggesting something (e.g. a knowledge or a teaching) that is available only for the specially initiated and secret from outsiders and perhaps even from ordinary believers.

Exorcism Removal of sin or evil, particularly an evil spirit in possession of someone, by prayer or ritual action.

F

Faith Attitude of belief, in trust and commitment to a divine being or a religious teaching. It can also refer to the beliefs of a religion, 'the faith', which is passed on from teachers to believers.

Fasting Total or partial abstinence from food, undertaken as a religious discipline. In indigenous religions it is often a preparation for a ceremony of initiation. It is also more generally used as a means of gaining clarity of vision and mystical insight.

Four stages of life Hindu outline of a man's ideal spiritual life. There are four stages (ashramas): student, the Hindu boy learns the scriptures in the house of his guru and lives a life of chastity; householder, he marries, has children and earns his living; retired life, when his family are grown up he gradually begins to withdraw from everyday life; renounced life, where he cuts all earthly ties and seeks liberation, often as a wandering beggar.

G

Gandhi (1869–1948 CE) Leader of the Indian independence movement and the greatest spiritual and political figure of modern India. Disowning violence, he advocated political change through non-violent resistance. After independence he tried to reconcile the Hindu and Muslim communities. He also campaigned against the social exclusion of Untouchables. He was assassinated by a Hindu nationalist.

Ganesha Elephant-headed god much loved in popular Hinduism, especially in western India. He is the god of good beginnings and is a symbol for luck and wealth in business and daily life.

Ganges The holy river of India whose waters are sacred for all Hindus. It is thought to flow from the toe of Vishnu. Pilgrims wash away evil in its waters and the ashes of the dead are thrown into it.

Ghat ('holy place') In Hindu use, a word which can refer to a range of hills, a ritual bathing place, or a cremation ground.

Guru ('teacher') A spiritual teacher or guide who, in Indian religion, awakens a disciple to a realization of his or her own divine nature.

A BRIEF INTRODUCTION TO HINDUISM

H

Hanuman Monkey-god of popular Hinduism. In the Ramayana he led a monkey army against a host of demons. He can fly and cover huge distances at great speed.

Hare Krishna Mantra used by devotees of Krishna to induce ecstatic union with the divine. The most familiar version is a two-line chant, invoking both Krishna and Rama. (*See also* International Society for Krishna Consciousness.)

Hell Realm where the wicked go after death. Religious teachings differ over whether this punishment is reformatory or eternal. Even religions which have a doctrine of reincarnation, such as Buddhism and Hinduism, include teachings about hells (although the belief in reincarnation makes them quite different from the teachings of Christianity and Islam).

Hindu Word used by Arabs to describe people living beyond the Indus Valley. Today it refers generally to people practising Indian religion who are neither Muslim, Sikh, Parsi, nor Jain, and also to their religion, Hinduism.

Hinduism A term coined by Europeans for a religious tradition and social system that emerged in India. It has no founder, no set creed, no prophets, and no single institutional structure. It is actually an umbrella term for an enormous range of beliefs and practices, from the worship of local village deities to the thought of a great philosopher such as Shankara. There are, however, some common beliefs which are basic to most strands of Hinduism. There is an emphasis on dharma (the right way of living) rather than assent to particular doctrines. Also found throughout Hinduism is the notion of moksha, or release from the eternal cycle of birth, death, and rebirth (samsara) to which one is bound by karma. Linked to this set of beliefs is the social stratification known as the caste system. The three chief Hindu deities are Brahma, Vishnu, and Shiva, who together form a triad known as the Trimurti. Numerous other deities are worshipped, but all are aspects of the universal spirit, Brahman. Hindus' concepts of God are complex and largely depends upon the Indian traditions and philosophy followed.. (*See also* Bhagavad Gita; brahman; Upanishads; Vedanta; Vedas.)

Holi Hindu spring festival which celebrates the love of Krishna and Radha. It is marked by boisterous games which are reminders of Krishna's amorous pranks with the cow-girls as told in the Mahabharata.

Holiness The sacred power, strangeness, and otherness of the divine.

Hymn A sacred song sung in the context of communal worship; a psalm of communal praise. Hymns are important in the gatherings of the Hindu bhakti cults.

I

Icon A likeness of a divine figure or saint painted on wood or inland in mosaic and used in public or private devotion.

Incarnation A term sometimes used for the Hindu doctrine of the avatar.

Incense Sweet-smelling smoke used in worship, made by burning certain aromatic substances.

Indigenous religions The preferred term for religions which are sometimes referred to as 'primal', 'tribal', 'traditional', 'primitive', and 'non-/pre-literate' religions. That said, indigenous religions are often developments of the traditional religions of tribal and aboriginal cultures. The problem with the earlier terminology was that it suggested simple, undeveloped, non-progressive, and archaic belief systems.

Indra Aryan god of war and storm. There are 200 hymns to him in the Rig Veda (*see* Vedas). He faded from significance in later Hinduism.

Initiation Ceremony marking coming of age, or entry into adult membership of a community. It is also used of the secret ceremonies surrounding membership of the mystery religions

International Society for Krishna Consciousness (ISKCON) Founded in 1965 by A. C. Bhaktivedanta Swami Prabhupada (1896–1977), and popularly known as the Hare Krishna movement, ISKCON is a modern bhakti cult which has been successful in Europe and America. Shaven-headed orange-robed devotees chant the mantra '*Hare Krishna*' as a way of reaching ecstatic union with God.

J

Judgment The divine assessment of individuals and the settling of their destinies, a notion found in many religions.

Jung, C. G. (Carl Gustav) (1875–1961 CE) Swiss psychiatrist who invented the theory of archetypes. He investigated the significance of myths, symbols, and dreams, and found in them evidence for a 'collective unconscious' which was at the root of religion.

K

Kabir (c. 1440–1518) Indian poet and hymn writer who influenced the development of early Sikhism. He attempted a synthesis of Islam and Hinduism, rejecting the caste system and circumcision, but teaching the love of God, rebirth, and liberation.

Kali Consort of the Hindu god Shiva, a black goddess who is portrayed with a necklace of human skulls and fangs dripping blood. She is both the goddess of destruction and the Great Mother, giver of life.

Kalki In Hindu tradition, the last avatar of Vishnu who will descend on a white horse, with a sword, to kill the wicked and bring the world to an end.

Kamma Pali word for karma.

Karma Sanskrit word for work or action. In Indian belief every action has inevitable consequences which attach themselves to the doer requiring reward or punishment. Karma is thus the moral law of cause and effect. It explains the inequalities of life as the consequences of actions in previous lives. The notion of karma probably developed among the Dravidian people of India. In Mahayana Buddhism the concept is transformed by the idea of the bodhisattva. Merit can be transferred by grace or faith, thus changing the person's karma.

Kashi *see* Benares.

Krishna The eighth incarnation of Vishnu according to Hindu tradition. His name means 'black'. Though of noble birth, he was brought up as a cowherd. Eventually he obtained his inheritance and ruled in justice. He was also a great lover: the Mahabharata describes his romances with the cow-girls which are seen as a type of God's love for the soul (I). He is also the main character in the Bhagavad Gita, where he appears disguised as the charioteer of Prince Arjuna.

Krishnamurti, Jiddhu (1895–1986) Indian spiritual teacher who was brought up by a leading Theosophist, Mrs Annie Besant, who proclaimed him as a World Teacher. He renounced this role in 1929 and became a solitary traveller, teaching liberation from dogma and organized religion by the rejection of belief in the individual ego. (*See also* Theosophy.)

Kshatriya *see* caste system.

Kundalini Energy that is coiled like a serpent at the base of the spine according to Tantrism. When awakened by yoga it leaps up the spine to the brain giving an experience of union and liberation re-enacting the sexual union of Shiva and Shakti.

L

Laity (from Greek *laos*, 'people') The non-ordained members of a religious community, or those with no specialist religious function.

Lakshmi Lord Vishnu's consort. She appears in the *Rig Veda* (*see* Vedas) as good fortune. In the Ramayana she rises out of the sea holding a lotus. She is involved in Vishnu's descents to earth as an avatar. Some associate her with Sita and Radha, the consorts of Rama and Krishna.

M

Madhva (1197–1276 CE) Indian philosopher who founded a dualist school (*see* dualism) in opposition to the monism of Shankara. He was a devotee of Vishnu, and believed that God was eternally distinct from the natural world. He may have been influenced by Christian teachings.

Magic The manipulation of natural or supernatural forced by spells and rituals for good or harmful ends.

Mahabharata One of the two great epics of the Hindu scriptures compiled by the third or second century BCE. Ascribed to the sage Vyasa, it tells of the war between two families, the Kauravas and the Pandus. The divine hero of the epic is the avatar Krishna.

Maharishi Mahesh Yogi *see* Transcendental Meditation.

Mahatma Sanskrit title of great respect or veneration meaning 'great soul'.

Mahatma Gandhi *see* Gandhi.

Mantra A symbolic sound causing an internal vibration which helps to concentrate the mind and aids self-realization, e.g. the repeated syllable 'om'. In Hinduism the term originally referred to a few sacred verses from the Vedas. It came to be thought that they possessed spiritual power, and that repetition of them was a help to liberation. A mantra is sometimes given by a spiritual teacher to a disciple as an initiation.

Mara In Buddhism, the evil one, temptation.

Maya (I) Illusion or deception in Hindu thought. *Maya* is concerned with the diverse phenomenal world perceived by the senses. It is the trick of *maya* to convince people that this is all that exists and thus blind them to the reality of brahman and the oneness of existence.

Meditation Deep and continuous reflection, practised in many religions with a variety of aims, e.g. to attain self-realization or, in theistic religions, to attain union with the divine will.

Medium One who is possessed by the spirit of a dead person or a divinity and, losing his or her individual identity, becomes the mouthpiece for the other's utterance.

Meher Baba (1894–1969 CE) Indian spiritual leader, regarded by his followers as an avatar. From 1925 until his death he did not speak once.

Miracle An event which appears to defy rational explanation and is attributed to divine intervention.

Mission The outreach of a religion to the unconverted. Whereas understandings of mission vary from faith to faith, the various aims of mission usually include spiritual conversion. However, mission is often conceived more holistically and concerns, not just spiritual conversion, but the transformation of all areas of life. It addresses injustice, suffering, poverty, racism, sexism, and all forms of oppression.

Moksha Sanskrit word meaning liberation from the cycle of birth, death, and rebirth. Permanent spiritual perfection experienced by

an enlightened soul after the physical body has died. No further incarnations will be endured.

Monism The belief that there is only one basic reality in spite of the appearance and experience of diversity. It applies particularly to the beliefs of the Hindu philosopher Shankara. (*See also* advaita.)

Monk A member of a male religious community living under vows which usually include poverty, chastity, and the wearing of a distinctive form of dress. Monastic orders are found in Christianity, Buddhism, Hinduism, and Jainism.

Monotheism The belief that there is one supreme God who contains all the attributes and characteristics of divinity.

Mother goddess/Great Mother The personification of nature and the natural processes of fertility and growth connected with the earth. Worship of a mother goddess was universal in the Ancient Near East, Asia, and Europe. Her worship continues in Hinduism, where the consorts of Shiva (Durga, Kali, Parvati) have some of her characteristics.

Mystic One who seeks direct personal experience of the divine and may use prayer, meditation or various ascetic practices to concentrate the attention.

Mysticism The search for direct personal experience of the divine. There is a distinction between seeing mysticism as leading to identification with God (as is common in Hinduism) and as leading to a union with God's love and will (as in Islam, Judaism, and Christianity).

Myth A sacred story which originates and circulates within a particular community. Some aetiological myths explain puzzling physical phenomena or customs, institutions and practices whose origin in the community would otherwise be mysterious.

N

Nature spirits Spirits of trees, hills, rivers, plants, and animals which are acknowledged with prayers and offerings in most indigenous religions.

Nibbana Pali word for nirvana.

Nirvana ('going out', 'becoming cool') In Buddhism, the state when dukkha ceases because the flames of desire are no longer fuelled. It is a state of unconditioned-ness and uncompounded-ness beyond any form of known or imagined existence.

Nun A member of a religious community of women, as found in Christianity, Buddhism, hinduism, and Jainism. Nuns live under vows usually including poverty, and chastity and often the wearing of a distinctive form of dress.

O

Occult Teachings, arts, and practices that are concerned with what is hidden and mysterious, as with witchcraft, alchemy, and divination.

Omnipotence All-powerful.

Omniscience All-knowing. Simultaneous knowledge of all things.

P

Pagan/Paganism The word 'pagan' (derived from the Latin term *pagus*, which literally means 'from the countryside' or 'rural') was first used in a general religious sense by the early Christians to describe the non-Christian gentile religions. It is now generally used to refer to a broad range of nature-venerating religious traditions.

Pantheism The belief that all reality is in essence divine.

Parvati ('mountaineer') Consort of Shiva, in Hindu mythology, like Shiva both beautiful and terrifying.

Philosophy of religion The branch of philosophy which investigates religious experience considering its origin, context, and value.

Pilgrimage A journey to a holy place, undertaken as a commemoration of a past event, as a celebration, or as an act of penance. The goal might be a natural feature such as a sacred river or mountain, or the location of a miracle, revelation, or theophany, or the tomb of a hero or saint.

Plato (c. 427–347 BCE) Greek philosopher and pupil of Socrates. He taught the theory of Forms or Ideas, which are eternal prototypes of the phenomena encountered in ordinary experience. Above all is the Form of the Good, which gives unity and value to all the forms. Plato also taught the immortality of the soul.

Polytheism The belief in and worship of a variety of gods, who rule over various aspects of the world and life.

Prayer The offering of worship, requests, confessions, or other communication to God or gods publicly or privately, with or without words; often a religious obligation.

Prehistoric religion Religions dating from the period before the development of writing.

Puja ('reverence') Refers to temple and domestic worship in Buddhism and Hinduism, and to the keeping of rites and ceremonies prescribed by the Brahmins (*see* caste system).

Puranas A vast corpus of sacred writings (c. 350–950 CE), which include mythologies of Hindu deities and avatars of Vishnu, the origins of the cosmos, and of humanity, pilgrimage, ritual, law codes, caste obligations, and so on. There are eighteen principal Puranas, each exalting a member of the *Trimurti* (Brahma, Vishnu, Shiva). They are very important in popular Hinduism, Jainism, and Buddhism, the most popular being the *Bhagavata Purana*, which deals with Krishna's early life and encourages devotion to him (bhakti).

R

Radha In Hinduism, friend and love of the god Vishnu as his avatar Krishna. The love of Krishna and Radha is a frequent theme of bhakti devotion where it is seen as a type of the love between God and the soul. The frank eroticism of the stories of Radha is not welcomed by all Hindus.

Radhakrishnan, Sarvepalli (1888–1975 CE) Indian philosopher who became vice-president and then president of India. He taught that there is a basic unity of all religions and that Hinduism is a useful meeting ground because of its breadth and tolerance.

Rama The seventh incarnation of Vishnu according to Hindu tradition. His exploits in love and war are described in the Ramayana. He is the epitome of righteousness and moral virtue.

Ramakrishna (1834–86 CE) Hindu Brahmin (*see* caste system) who taught that all religions are paths to the same goal. He laid the foundation of Hindu universalism. He was a devotee of Kali, though philosophically he adhered to the teaching of Shankara.

Ramakrishna Mission Indian religious order founded in 1897 by Vivekananda. Its aims are to teach Vedanta and to care for the sick and needy. It has dispensaries, libraries and welfare centres throughout India and has teaching branches in Europe and the USA.

Ramanuja (d. 1137 CE) Indian philosopher who opposed Shankara's stress on the oneness of being and denied that the divine lord belonged to a lower order of reality. He believed God and the world were related like body and soul, inseparable but distinct. He was a devotee of Vishnu, and believed in the validity of personal devotion to God.

Ramayana One of the two great epics of the Hindu scriptures compiled in the second or first century BCE. Ascribe to the sage Valmiki, it tells of the life of the avatar Rama.

Rammohan Roy (1772–1833 CE) Hindu reformer who founded the Brahmo Samaj, an ethical organization with monotheistic tendencies, in opposition to the idolatry of popular devotion. He believed the Vedas taught monotheism, though he also used Christian and Muslim ideas.

Reincarnation The belief that individual souls survive death and are reborn to live again in a different body, thus passing through a series of lives. Held in pre-Aryan India, the belief is associated with the doctrine of karma. Some traditions believe rebirth is possible only in human bodies, others envisage hellish or heavenly states, while others suggest a transmigration in which human souls are tied to animal or vegetable forms. Some Hindu apologists explain the doctrine as a mythical way of speaking about the continuity of the human race.

Relics Bones or remains of saints, venerated and accredited with miraculous powers in many religions.

Religion (from Latin religare, 'to tie something tightly') A system of belief and worship, held by a community who may express its religion through shared myths, doctrines, ethical teachings, rituals, or the remembrance of special experiences.

Renunciation Giving up ownership of material possessions.

Rita The cosmic order as understood in the Hindu Vedas. It is the principle of ethical and physical organization throughout the universe and is the work of the sky god Varuna.

Rites of passage Religious ceremonies which mark the transition from one state of life to another. In many religions these transitional periods are felt to be dangerous and to require spiritual protection. Examples include birth rites, initiation rites, marriage rites, and funeral rites.

Ritual Religious ceremonial performed according to a set pattern of words, movements, and symbolic actions. Rituals may involve the dramatic re-enactment of ancient myths featuring gods and heroes, performed to ensure the welfare of the community.

S

Sacred Thread ceremony Initiation ceremony performed on Hindu and Buddhist boys. A sacred thread is placed around the neck indicating that the boy is one of the twice-born and has entered the first stage of life. (*See also* navjote.)

Sacrifice The ritual offering of animal or vegetable life to establish communion between humans and a god or gods.

Sai Baba (1926–2011 CE) Spiritual teacher from south India who is regarded by his followers as an avatar. Probably the most popular and influential guru in present-day India, he specialized in curing illness and materializing gifts for his disciples.

Saint Holy person or dead hero of faith who is venerated by believers on earth and held to be a channel of divine blessing.

Salvation In Eastern religions, release from the changing material world to identification with the absolute.

Samsara ('stream of existence') Sanskrit word which refers to the cycle of birth and death followed by rebirth as applied both to individuals and to the universe itself.

Sanctuary A place consecrated to a god, a holy place, a place of divine refuge and

protection. Also, the holiest part of a sacred place or building. Historically, in some cultures, a holy place where pursued criminals or victims were guaranteed safety.

Sannyasi ('one who renounces') The last of the Hindu Four Stages of Life.

Sanskrit The language of the Aryan peoples and of the Hindu scriptures. It is an Indo-European language related to Latin, Greek, and Persian.

Sarasvati In Hinduism, the goddess of truth and consort of Brahma, the Creator.

Satguru In popular Hinduism a term for a revered teacher such as Sai Baba.

Scripture Writings which are believed to be divinely inspired or especially authoritative within a particular religious community.

Sect A group, usually religious (but it can be political), which has separated itself from an established tradition, claiming to teach and practise a truer form of the faith from which it has separated itself. It is, as such, often highly critical of the wider tradition which it has left.

Shaivism Worship of the Hindu god Shiva and his family. It is particularly strong in southern India and appeals to extreme ascetics.

Shakti ('energy', 'power') A feminine word, particularly associated with Shiva and his consorts (*see* Durga; Kali; Parvati). In Tantrism *shakti* is universal creativity and exists in people as a latent energy located at the base of the spine (*see* kundalini). In tantric yoga this energy is awakened to travel up the spine and unite with Shiva, who is present as mind.

Shankara (788–820 CE) The best-known exponent of classical Hindu philosophy. Developing the thought of the Upanishads, he declared that only the eternal being is real; the diverse, phenomenal world is an illusion of maya. Even the notion of a personal God is part of maya. Liberation comes from realizing oneness with the absolute, which is defined as Being, Consciousness, and Bliss.

Shiva One of the great gods of Hindu devotion. He is a god of contrasts, presiding over creation and destruction, fertility and asceticism, good, and evil. He is the original Lord of the Dance who dances out the creation of the universe. As god of ascetics he is portrayed as a great *yogi*, smeared with

ashes, holding the world in being through meditation. His symbol is a phallus-shaped pillar denoting procreation.

Shudras *see* caste system.

Sikh ('disciple') Follower of the Sikh religion which developed in the fifteenth century CE in northern India as a synthesis of Islam and Hinduism. (*See also* Adi Granth; Gobindh Singh; Gurdwara; Kabir; Khalsa; Nanak; Singh.)

Sin An action which breaks a divine law.

Sita Consort of Rama in Hindu tradition.

Socrates (469–399 BCE) Greek philosopher and teacher and mentor of Plato. He taught by a method of question and answer which sought to elicit a consistent and rational response and hence to arrive at a universally agreed truth.

Soma The juice of the Indian *soma* plant, which may have been fermented or had hallucinogenic properties. It was drunk by gods and men in the Vedas, and was regarded as a mediating god with power over all plants and as a conveyor of immortality.

Sorcerer A practitioner of harmful magic. In indigenous religions sorcerers are sometimes believed to be able to kill others through magic.

Soteriology Teaching about salvation.

Soul (1) The immortal element of an individual man or woman which survives the death of the body in most religious teachings. (2) A human being when regarded as a spiritual being.

Spell A formula of words with or without accompanying ritual actions which is believed to have the power to manipulate natural or supernatural forces for good or evil ends.

Spiritualism Any religious system or practice which has the object of establishing communication with the dead.

Swami General term for a Hindu holy man or member of a religious order.

Swaminarayan (1781–1830 CE) Gujarati preacher and founder of a popular sect which attracted Sikh and Hindu followers.

Syncretism The growing together of two or more religions making a new development in religion which contains some of the beliefs and practices of both.

T

Tagore, Rabindranath (1861–1941 CE)
Bengali poet, playwright, musician, and
Nobel prize-winner, whose passionate
espousal of Bengali culture influenced the
cause of Indian nationalism.

Tat tvam asi ('you are that') Phrase from the
Upanishads which expresses the claim that
brahman, the divine power sustaining the
universe, and atman, the soul, are one.

Temple Building designed for worship of
God or gods, usually containing a sanctuary
or holy place where sacrifice may be offered.

Theism The belief in one supreme God
who is both transcendent and involved in the
workings of the universe.

Theology A systematic formulation of
belief made by or on behalf of a particular
individual or church or other body of
believers.

Theophany A divine appearance, revelation,
or manifestation, usually inducing awe and
terror in those who witness it. For example,
the appearance of Krishna in his divine form,
'like a thousand suns', as described in the
Bhagavad Gita.

Theosophy ('divine wisdom') A term applied
to various mystical movements but which
refers particularly to the principles of the
Theosophical Society founded by Madame
Blavatsky in 1875. These comprise a
blend of Hindu, Buddhist, and Christian
ideas, together with particular stress on
reincarnation, immortality, and the presence
of God in all things.

Transcendent That which is above or beyond
common human experience or knowledge.

Transcendental Meditation/TM Meditation
technique taught by Maharishi Mahesh Yogi
which has flourished in the West since the
1960s. Practitioners need no religious beliefs.
They are taught to meditate for fifteen to
twenty minutes twice a day; this reduces stress
and aids relaxation. In some states in the
USA it has been ruled that Transcendental
Meditation is a religion, of Hindu origin.

Transmigration of souls The belief held by
some Hindus that souls are detached from
their bodies at death and are attached to
other human, animal, or vegetable bodies.
What the new body will be depends on the
individual's karma.

Trimurti The three principal deities in
Hinduism – Brahma, Vishnu, and Shiva, who
are believed to control the three activities –
creation, preservation, and destruction –
inherent in the created cosmos.

U

Untouchables Indians who belong to no caste
(see caste system) and are therefore banished
from normal social life. Mahatma Gandhi
called them 'children of God' and worked for
their acceptance in Indian society.

Upanishads The last books of the Indian
vedas which were written in Sanskrit between
800 and 400 BCE. They develop the concept
of brahman as the holy power released in
sacrifice to the point where it becomes the
underlying reality of the universe. The soul,
atman, is identified with the holy power,
Brahman. They include speculation on how
the soul can realize its oneness with Brahman
through contemplative techniques.

V

Vaishnavism Worship of, or devotion to, the
Hindu god Vishnu. Devotees regard him as
the sole deity, of whom other gods are mere
aspects.

Vaishyas see caste system.

Varanasi see Benares.

Varuna Indian sky god of the Vedic period
(see Vedas). He produced the cosmic order
and was seen as a heavenly ruler and lawgiver
as well as a moral guardian of the earth.

Vedanta (1) 'The end of the Vedas'. A name
for the Upanishads, which close the period
of Hindu revelation. (2) Indian philosophy
based on the teachings of Shankara. Its basic
tenet is that only Brahman, the Absolute,
is fully real. The world of sense experience
is contradictory and dreamlike because it is
spun from the illusions of maya (1). Release
from illusion comes from recognizing the
sole reality of Brahman.

Vedas Scriptures which express the religion
of the Aryan people of India. They
comprise hymns, instructions for ritual,
and cosmological speculations. There are
four divisions: *Rig Veda*, hymns to the Aryan
gods who are personifications of natural
forces; *Sama Veda*, verses selected for chanting
(see chant); *Yajur Veda*, prose instructions on

matters of ritual; *Atharva Veda*, rites and spells
in verse, especially concerned with curing
illness.

Vishnu In Hinduism, the divine as preserver
and life-giver, the creator of the cosmos. He
and Shiva are the two great gods of Hindu
devotion. As lawgiver and moral guardian,
Vishnu appears on earth from time to time
as an avatar to reawaken people to knowledge
of truth.

Vivekananda (1863–1902) Follower
of Ramakrishna and founder of the
Ramakrishna Mission in 1897. An apologist
for Vedanta, he criticized the dogmatism
of Christianity. Attending the World's
Parliament of Religions in Chicago in 1893,
he commended Vedanta as the highest form
of religion.

W

Witch doctor/Medicine man A healer in
indigenous religions. The terms are rarely
used today as they are felt to have misleading
connotations.

Worship Reverence or homage to God or
a god which may involve prayer, sacrifice,
rituals, singing, dancing, or chanting.

Y

Yama In the Vedas the primordial man who
crosses through death and becomes immortal.
He is therefore god of death who judges men
and consigns them to heaven or hell. His
significance as judge faded as the pre-Aryan
doctrine of Samsara became established.

Yoga A way to union with God in Hindu
philosophy. It also forms one of the
six classical systems of Indian thought.
Traditionally there are eight stages of yoga:
restraint, discipline, posture, breathing,
detachment, concentration, meditation, and
trance. In the Bhagavad Gita the three paths
to spiritual fulfilment are: jnanayoga (the path
of knowledge/wisdom), karmayoga (the path
of work/action), and bhaktiyoga (the path
of devotion).

Yogi Indian holy man who has reached
enlightenment through yogic practices (see
yoga). (See also Transcendental Meditation.)

Index

Numbers in **bold type** indicate pages with illustrations.
The Rapid Fact-Finder is not indexed.

Picture Acknowledgments

Dreamstime pp. 16, 29, 38, 41, 44, 72, 76, 78, 79, 92

Illustrated London News pp. 13, 32, 61

Photodisc p. 25

Photolink pp. 68, 69

Tim Dowley Associates pp. 35, 86